D0626764

2/20

in the weather of the heart

also by valerie monroe

CITYKIDS (with susan haven)

DOUBLEDAY

new york

london

toronto

sydney

auckland

in the *weather* of the *heart*

a memoir
of a
shattered
marriage
and a
reckoning
with
recovery

valerie monroe

PUBLISHED BY DOUBLEDAY
a division of Bantam Doubleday Dell Publishing Group, Inc.
1540 Broadway, New York, New York 10036

DOUBLEDAY and the portrayal of an anchor with a
dolphin are trademarks of Doubleday, a division of
Bantam Doubleday Dell Publishing Group, Inc.

Book design by Susan Yuran

Library of Congress Cataloging-in-Publication Data

Monroe, Valerie.
In the weather of the heart: a memoir of a shattered marriage and
a reckoning with recovery / Valerie Monroe.
p.   cm.
1. Suicide—United States—Case studies.   2. Monroe, Valerie.
3. Twins—United States—Case studies.   I. Title.
HV6548.U5M66   1996
155.9′37—dc20   95-53090   CIP

ISBN 0-385-47103-3

July 1996

1   2   3   4   5   6   7   8   9   10

FIRST EDITION

for keith,
whose story this is
as much as mine

and to the memory
of my father, arthur "red" monroe
1913–79

acknowledgments

For their support during the writing of this book, my deep thanks to Christina Ferrari, Anne Conover Heller, and Anita Diamant. Some wise thing Susan Allen Toth said during the course of a long phone conversation was the catalyst that started me writing. Gail Hochman's friendship and enthusiasm gave me the courage to keep writing. David James Duncan's magnificent essay, "A Mickey Mantle Koan" (*Harper's,* September 1992), inspired me to try to tell my story with as much clarity and hope. Deb Futter valiantly read the manuscript many times, and always offered helpful insights. Betsy Lerner caught the nearly finished book on a pass and ran with it, and for that I feel both lucky and grateful. Ann Manca offered patient assistance on the computer.

Rick, thanks always for your constancy along the edge. Marilou, thank you for enriching my perspective, in every way. Reid, thank you for your smart suggestions, for your unrelenting insistence on accuracy—and for hanging up your jacket. And Keith, I could never have written this book if you hadn't supported it, and me. Thanks.

This book is a reconstruction of the past as I remember it; or, in two cases when I obviously wasn't present, as I imagined it.

I've changed the names and identities of some people to protect their privacy.

in the weather of the heart

1

The photographs, twenty of them or more, lay in neat lines across the kitchen table. The three of us stared at them, amazed. Keith had grouped them by year, so that what we saw was a spare chronology of the two brothers' lives. Keith and Brian, identical twins, impossibly fat toddlers at two. Grammar school head shots of freckled five-year-olds, the sweet padded cheeks of babyhood not yet lost. Then third-graders, holding the same self-effacing gaze, heads turned slightly from the camera, identically uncomfortable. Same clothes, same haircuts, same face, year after year, through an ungainly adolescence and into high school. Two newly handsome boys on a sloping lawn, sharing an impatient posture, squinting into the sun. Brian and Keith. Keith and Brian. Which one was which?

Keith—my husband—could not tell. Memory wouldn't serve him at all. Because the twins' mother, or an aunt, had marked the pictures on the back, we didn't have to live with the mystery, but it was interesting to try to guess. I had no better luck than Keith. It was our six-year-old son, looking at the photos with unprecedented concentration, who began to point, one by one, at the photographs of his father. "Daddy," he said, touching the image of the toddler climbing down from the sofa. *Keith, climbing down* read the inscription on the back. "Daddy," said our son, putting his small finger on the photo of the five-year-old on the right. *Keith, r.* read the back. "Daddy. Daddy. Daddy," said Reid, fingering one photograph and then the next. On every one, he was right.

Was it luck? Or a focus extended from some unnameable connection between my husband and our son? Did Reid, seeing his father from the particular, unique vantage point of being his child, possess a kind of sixth sense about him? I savored the idea of a connection, hoping that it was powerful, hoping that my husband's strengths—his belief in himself, his unflinching honesty, his determination about doing what he thought was right—would nourish our son, feed his spirit, protect him from despair. Looking at Reid's face, which resembled the twins' young faces, indistinguishable, open, expectant, I felt a dull, aching sadness. "Do you remember Uncle Brian?" I asked him. He looked off into the room for a minute, thinking. "I don't know," he said. "When did he die?"

My husband and I looked at each other as if the answer would materialize in the air between us. When Keith didn't speak, I softly said, "You were just a baby, I guess." But the silence then seeped back between us and grew, gathering presence and meaning and a weird, ubiquitous energy. Sensing its power, I realized: Brian's death, the fact of it, was not, was never a finite thing, but an influence that lived in us, in Keith and me and even in Reid, its effects expanding even as we moved, in time, away from it.

Keith and I do not completely agree about how Brian died. Neither one of us will ever know exactly what happened; I believe that it doesn't really matter.

Eleven years ago, and three years into our marriage. The call came one morning, on our bedroom phone, on the number only our families had, and a few good friends. Even before I had the idea that something was wrong, my heart, aware, skipped with the irregular beat of fear; as I pressed the phone to my ear, the fuzzy connection hissed and sputtered with faraway static. An unfamiliar voice, cracking sharply through, asked for Keith.

"It's six o'clock in the morning, you know," I said. "Who is this?"

"I have to speak to him."

Keith, next to me, was up on one elbow. I wish I could stop this right now, I thought, glancing over at him. I wish I could hang up the phone and this man would not call back and we would never know what we are about to find out. My marriage was tough enough as it was; I didn't want to have to deal with one more difficult thing. The room was cool, and I pulled the quilt up over my shoulders as Keith took the phone from my hand.

"This is Keith," he said, sitting up. He listened. "Are you sure it's him?" he said. "Where did it happen? Are you sure it's him?" His hand shook as he ran it through his hair.

"Are you sure he's dead?" he said.

On one of those wide, nondescript white highways, where driving is always only a way to get from one place to the next, where the clean, uncluttered lanes quietly invite speed and dreamy contemplation, Brian will crash his car. He floors the accelerator, feels the shimmy of the wheel, as if the car has just begun to skim the surface of the road, as if it might suddenly rise up with a bump like a light plane off the highway and careen unsteadily into the air. He sees a concrete abutment coming up fast, cuts sharply toward it, but he hits the shoulder, or the low mound of an embankment, and then another bump and another more violent one, knocking him off course. He slams the brake, throwing himself forward. There is the long, deep groan of metal crunching and a sharp exclamation of shattering glass. And then silence, and the soft tick, tick, ticking of the engine cooling off.

Brian sits at the wheel. He wrenches open the door. Kicks it open with his bare foot. He is wearing only shorts, no shirt and no shoes, and the air outside the car is cool and sweet with the green smell of the fields along the highway. A low hum rises from the road. . . .

It is very early morning, the time when cold and dark blanket the ground and, if you're driving, make you feel as if you're going nowhere, as if you're traveling on faith alone. Cars, their icy headlights slicing a way through the night, slip by left and right, fluid, inky. With ferocious purpose, the howling eighteen-wheelers bear down and overtake you in great shuddery gusts.

Standing by the side of the highway, unmoving, Brian looks down the road. One of those monsters is coming now, barreling west, with unconscious speed. He watches it approach, calculating. And when it's close enough that he can begin to feel the thunder of its heavy rolling power, clearly see the sharp, steely tusks of its diesel smoke-ducts, he dashes into the road in a wild, propulsive sprint. Bounces with a loud dead thud against the grille. Kills himself instantly, on impact.

The coroner's report: July 23, 1985. White male. Age last birthday: 36. Immediate cause of death: traumatic skull fracture with laceration of brain. Interval between onset of injury and death: immediate. Other significant conditions contributing to death: rupture of aorta, liver, spleen, multiple rib fractures. Describe how injury occurred: Jumped in front of truck. Death due to: Suicide.

"You know, I can't remember exactly when Brian died," I said to Keith one night not long ago. Though I have kept a detailed calendar for more than ten years, I made no indication, no notation of Brian's death or any of the events surrounding it. I had to guess the year, figuring out how old Reid was when it happened, and then I combed through that year's calendar, finding nothing. I was afraid to write anything down, as if by marking it, the tragedy would worm its way into my life, as if I could contain its effects by not acknowledging it.

"It was 1985," I said to Keith, "but I can't remember what season it was."

"July," Keith said firmly. Then losing hold of his conviction, "Maybe the end of July. Or early August."

Then I remembered the gorgeous, warm sunny morning we packed up some things, Reid's baby bag, his bottles, a few toys— like a happy young family, going on a picnic—stowed everything into a rented car, clean and brand new, and drove the forty miles to the New Jersey hospital where Keith would identify Brian's body.

I knew that one of the highways we would take was the same one that Brian had died on the night before. Even as I hoped that there would be no evidence of the accident—skid marks, a sneaker lying on its side, a bloodstain, thick and sticky, shimmering on the grass—I scanned the road as we sailed past, looking, I suppose, for something that would help to make what had happened seem real to me. Since the phone call that morning, I had begun to feel completely disconnected from what I was doing, as if I were playacting in somebody else's life.

Keith, quiet, pale, his hands gripping the steering wheel, looked only straight ahead.

Finally, we swung onto the exit for the hospital. "That was around where it happened," Keith said hoarsely. Though the air conditioner in the car was on high, deep circles of perspiration darkened his shirt under his arms.

Why did we bring the baby? I ask myself now. Why didn't I leave him with a neighbor or a friend? Though Keith had suggested that I stay home, rather than bring Reid, and he would go alone, I couldn't bear that idea. But neither could I bear being separated from Reid while confronting the fear that Brian's death aroused in me. From the time Keith and I had been married, I had felt increasingly estranged from him, and I didn't know why. His quietness, which was one of the qualities that had initially attracted me to him, had become a curtain between us, more layered and opaque with time.

I needed to have Reid near me, needed to feel the practical, fundamental satisfaction of administering to him. Reid was a buffer against my fear; all that long morning and afternoon he kept me occupied with the business of life, with a one-and-a-half-year-old's incessant demands, while Keith numbly took care of the business at hand.

The great lawn of the hospital grounds yawned wide and green. Reid and I planted ourselves in a sunny spot on the soft grass to watch ants and dig with little sticks. A guard approached us, preparing to ask us to move; the grass was not for sitting on.

"We're just waiting here, we won't be long," I said apologetically. I gestured toward the hospital building. "My husband's in the morgue."

"Sorry," the guard said, shaking his head and walking quickly on, "sorry."

Inside the hospital, Keith and I, with Reid on my hip, had been led down the stark white hallways to the morgue. I went with him as far as I dared to, but had to wait in the hall while he went into the room where Brian's body lay. I knew I couldn't handle seeing him. After a few moments, Keith returned, his face and his lips absolutely bloodless, white as the walls. He had that tentative walk of the light-headed or snow-blinded, as if he were feeling his way along uneven ground. I thought he might faint.

"Are you okay?" I asked him.

"I'm okay."

I would have embraced him, but I was holding Reid, who was trying to put his hand inside my mouth. Instinctively, I pulled my face away, held him by the wrist, and wiped his fingers on my shirt. "What did he look like?"

Keith shook his head. "It's amazing," he said hesitantly, with the reverence you use for describing an awesome natural disaster. He put one hand on the wall to steady himself and closed his eyes. "One side of his body—I think it's the right side—one side of his body's all caved in and he's been sewn up with this heavy black thread like a doll. . . .

"He was hit by a truck?" Keith asked suddenly, turning to one of the men who accompanied us downstairs. "He must have been hit by a truck?"

"Yes, that's right," one of them said, and then said gently that Keith needed to talk to someone in the hospital and fill out some papers and would I like to go upstairs while he got that done? I looked at Keith, who nodded. Relieved, I threaded my way back quickly through the maze of sterile corridors, the smell of disinfectant dank and sour in my nostrils, till I reached the smoky glass entrance doors, which I burst through with a shudder into the sun.

To Keith, emerging later from the cool white light of the morgue, the flashy glint of the sun on the police car and the officer's buttons and buckles seemed gaudy, artificial, and strange. This is not my life, he thought ironically; my life is down there in the room where Brian lies, dead and naked and sewn together—and real—in a way nothing else seems to be. A couple of policemen wanted to talk to Keith; was it okay if they asked him some questions?

"Do you think your brother was involved with drugs?" one of them asked.

"Yes," Keith said. For months before he died, Brian had plagued Keith with phone calls: he was shooting cocaine, he wanted to stop, he couldn't do it alone, he was going into rehab, he was kicked out of rehab. He was thinking of suicide. One night he'd phoned Keith and told him that he had held a gun to his head. "What should I do?" Keith had said to me, in a whisper that hardly concealed his desperation. "What should I do?" He leaned with both hands open against the kitchen table, as if he were bearing down on his fear, as if it might pop up like a fist on a coiled spring and clutch him by the heart.

"He's not going to shoot himself," I'd told Keith. "He's bluffing." I was sure of it. I resented the time Keith spent trying to help Brian; he seemed to ask for help only to reject it.

Now one of the cops was asking, "Do you think that he might have taken his own life?"

"Yes."

"Do you know that he had tried to take his life before?"

Keith felt a jolt, the sudden opening of a trapdoor that dropped him into a belly-sickening black slide. He closed his eyes, stiffened, and curled his fingers tight in his pockets. "No. When?"

A month and a half earlier, the police told him, Brian had deliberately crashed his car into an abutment and had to be admitted to this hospital for minor injuries. His girlfriend had come for him; his family was never notified.

That was the first time, Keith says, that he had the tormenting, crushing, and finally, intolerable idea that he might have done something to save Brian's life.

But how could he have saved Brian? And how could he *not* have saved him? These were the questions that tyrannized Keith.

My heart fills up with sympathy and compassion for my husband now, when I think of him on that day. I never asked him, *What did you feel, looking down into your twin brother's face?* Frightened of inviting his grief into my life, some strong admonition had risen up in me, warning me about his real feelings, and my own. I could only share as much of his sadness as I could imagine. So we moved on, separately, trying to manage our pain and fear.

Years later, at the invitation of a mother of a child in Reid's school, I met with a group of four women one morning for a kind of informal discussion group. By the end of the morning, the conversation had turned, inevitably, toward our work. One of the women asked what I was writing. "A book about my marriage . . ." I began, reluctant to get into the whole story. "My husband's identical twin killed himself, and then my husband got very sick." Another woman quickly asked, "Did your husband survive?" Yes, I told her.

"I was married to an identical twin whose brother killed himself, too," she said. "My husband died eighteen months later, of cancer. I read somewhere that it's not unusual for the second twin to die within that period of time. You're lucky."

In the thick silence that followed her remarks I remembered what a neighbor had told me just after she'd heard that Brian had died: that—in terms of the grief—losing an identical twin can be more devastating than losing a parent, a sibling, even a child. That I'd better watch Keith carefully. That he had suffered the deepest kind of loss imaginable.

How can one move through that? I wondered.

Is it possible?

2

Before we were married, when his design studio was small and he was still delivering his own work, Keith rode his bicycle to see his clients. In the late spring and summer he would often meet me at my magazine job at the end of the day and walk me home, with one arm around my waist and the other maneuvering his bike through the evening crowd. The dense city heat rising off the streets hit us in thick, vaporous puffs, as if it were being pumped up from a giant engine underground. I loved the feeling of Keith's hand on my hip, the warmth and the life of it through the cool, indifferent fabric of my summer dress. When he needed both hands to guide his bike over a curb or across the street, I felt bare on the spot where he had been holding me; I wasn't completely comfortable until he slid his arm around me again.

He struck me as immensely handsome and immensely shy. I had never actually known anyone as shy as he. I had run into him one afternoon on the street by chance, after not having seen him for six years since we had left the magazine where we had both worked. I was surprised again by how quiet he was. Not timid; reticent. He seemed taken aback by my straightforwardness and delighted by it, and not quite sure how to respond. Looking at him, I could see that there was something going on behind his face, some kind of figuring-out, but I couldn't tell what it was.

During the months that we worked together, we probably had no more than a couple of hours of conversation. It was my first real job, and the first years of an exciting magazine, and the place was exhilarating and chaotic. There was plenty to think about at the office besides a *man*. But I was terribly attracted to him, and the difficulty I had talking to him only added to the sexual tension I felt.

The first time I saw him, I was leaving the office as he was coming in. I remember that he had a bandana tied over his long hair, covering his forehead and knotted in the back. He looked kind of roguish, or defiant. (Keith denies that he ever wore a bandana, but that is the way I remember him.) He carried his portfolio, a large, black, flat, square affair. We looked one another in the eye as we passed, a look so loaded that it stopped me. I literally couldn't take another step away from him. His eyes were wide and clear and slate gray, and seemed to take in everything all at once in their gaze, not squinched up like some men's, which made them look as if they were protecting themselves from the sun or some other bright object. After I was sure he'd gone into the office, I turned around and went back in myself, as if I'd forgotten something and had to return to retrieve it. I ran into my girlfriend as I headed back to my desk.

"Whoa," she said, walking with me. "Who is *that?*"

"Don't know yet, but I'm going to find out," I said as I opened my desk drawer and pretended to rummage. My friend faced away from me, where she could still see him.

"Shit," she said suddenly. "I think he's the new guy in the art department."

"He is?" I said, looking up. "Wow, that's great," I said as I turned so that I could see him talking with the art director. "I could really use a good layout."

"Hardy-har," my friend said.

He was married, then, to a woman he'd gone to college with, and I chalked up his lack of follow-through to my friendliness to fidelity. My desk was near the art department, where I was able to watch him as he moved around in a kind of careful dance with the infamous, often irascible art director. His eyes betrayed nothing of the irritation she must have aroused in him.

The magazine, staffed almost entirely by women, funny, smart, aggressive women hashing out the complexities of the feminist movement—and a mother lode of their own neuroses—wasn't exactly a hothouse for romantic love. At least not of the heterosexual kind. Keith kept his distance. What he did notice was the atmosphere ("very charged") and me ("nice ass"). He wisely kept his observations to himself.

On the street that afternoon years later I gave Keith a peck on the cheek and said, "Call me," as we went our separate ways, really meaning it, but not expecting to hear from him.

He phoned me at work—by then I had moved to a different magazine—after a couple of weeks. "I'd like to see you," he said.

"Oh, that's good," I'd told him, without hiding my surprise. I started flipping through my appointment book. "Lunch next Thursday?"

"Tomorrow would be better," he said.

"Tomorrow?" I laughed. "But I can't have lunch with you tomorrow."

"Dinner, then."

"Jeez, well . . . dinner would be hard. How about a drink?"

"If that's the best you can do."

So he met me on his bike after work and we went into a bar across the street, and in the pastel banquette he became his shy self again. But I slowly began to see another side of him, too, the side that gave him the confidence to put the rush on me.

He had just recently moved into a loft space, he said, that he'd bought with his wife. It wasn't finished, but he had been working and sleeping there, while his wife stayed in their old apartment. They had been separated for three months, he told me, and now he was sure it was the right thing. Though it had been coming for a long time, they had been together for a long time, too, and he knew that a divorce would be painful.

Uh-oh, I thought. I was in a serious relationship with a man who would never divorce his wife. Maybe I'd better wait this one out, I thought, as I listened to Keith. But I knew I wouldn't: some need pulled me inexorably into the drama.

Keith looked at me as if he were trying to read my mind. "No, really, it's happening," he said.

It did happen, and the separation process was protracted and painful, and Keith was sick with guilt. He was unhappy enough in his marriage to be sure he wanted a divorce, he said, but he couldn't stand the idea of hurting his wife. He punished himself with her unhappiness. Once, he tried to talk to me about his own sadness. "I'm sorry," he said, not wanting to burden me with his feelings, "but this is really hard." He took my hand and his eyes filled up. He wasn't sure if he could cry in front of me, and I wasn't going to encourage him. At my stony look, he turned his face away, but he held my hand for a moment longer, as if he still hoped to squeeze some compassion out of it. We were in bed, it was late, and I had had a couple of drinks. I felt selfish and impatient. I wanted to close the book on that part of his life. "Oh, get over it," I snapped, and pulled my hand away. When I saw how wounded he was, I felt still angrier. I didn't like another woman having such a powerful effect on him. On the day his divorce came through he called me to tell me that congratulations were in order. Then he ran into the john and vomited.

Well, I thought, maybe he's finally got that out of his system.

Five months after our later meeting, I moved in with him. I adored him. He used to leave me little notes all over the house. A small, pink cardboard heart, inscribed, *I love you, my angel. K.* A yellow Post-it on my desk, on my pillow, on my coffee cup: *I love you, Angelou. I love you, my little peach tree. I love you, my ripe tomato. I love you, Val Monroe.*

He did love me, and I knew it.

"I like the way you look when you're asleep," he told me one morning just after we'd awakened and were cuddling in bed. I cringed. I felt as if someone had come into my house and examined my things while I was gone. In my flight to a rich and vivid dreamworld, I abandoned my body like a discarded husk; I hated the idea of looking inert.

"But you look so peaceful," Keith said, "and you always have the sweetest smile. . . ." He traced my lips lightly with his finger. Then he kissed me.

"You prince," I whispered as we embraced.

I couldn't get enough of him. My physical attraction to him was uncontained, unwieldy. When we'd first become lovers, I'd staggered around with it, trying to put it away at work or during conversations with my friends, but it tumbled around inside me, knocking over all my other feelings, leaving me in a pleasant, intoxicated state of emotional dishevelment. Though, as Keith and I spent more time together, there began to be lapses in the continuity of that feeling (unquestionably a relief), the intensity did not abate. His quietness, his privateness made me want to open myself to him. I felt safe with him; despite the excitement of a new relationship, I sensed, beneath the thrill, a loyal, steady presence. I wanted to take him in, to include him in my secrets, to watch him as he watched me unfold.

He was never satisfied until he had pleased me, and he knew how. It was this knowingness and a kind of gravity—not just about me, but about everything—that made me desire him.

His gravity both rooted him and made him vulnerable; it was as if he had never accrued the defenses, the social armature that most of us acquired as we grew up; as if he were completely uncorrupted. He endured being with new people socially for my sake, but it unnerved him. At dinner parties, over the course of an evening, I would watch with a mixture of baffled amusement and concern as he gradually assumed a stiff, tormented posture: a Munster in Armani. On our way home, I would try patting his shoulders down. "Relax!" I'd tell him. "It's supposed to be fun!" But I could see that for him, walking into a candlelit room full of people he didn't know was like stepping into the flickering hellfire of Satan's palace, the noisy chatter a chthonic opera.

Does it make sense when I say that there was an elegance in the way he looked at things? I loved the way he saw the world. Watching him work out a design, watching the clean, precise movements that brought it eventually together fascinated me. And another thing: he was able to tune out the distracting static to which I often gravitated, the interesting gossip, the drama of our friends' and colleagues' lives, and focus on even the simplest task with an absorption that combined concentration and a sense of wonder and appreciation. I envied his ability to fall headlong into his work as if he were falling into a trance, his total lack of need of outside motivation or appreciation, the way he was happily unconcerned about what people thought of what he did. He had no interest in the kind of needful ambition I saw in many of our friends; he didn't care about being among the first-to-know, and he shunned the empty acquisitiveness that both disgusted and attracted me about living in New York. The silence that made him seem reserved socially, transformed him when he was involved in his work or pursuing any of his projects; it became, instead of a holding-back, a well, brimming with his concentration and enjoyment. He was largely uninterested and out of touch with the real world—once he asked me, "Who the hell is this Jerry Steinfield guy, anyway?"—but in his interior world, Keith was abundantly content.

I recognized this state of being in Keith; I craved it. I shared it, too, but it was not as accessible to me. As a kid, I was blissful in the midst of solitude; it was as if I had slipped into another dimension, penetrated an invisible wall that separated hard, rocklike reality from another one more alive, where ordinary things pulsed and shimmered and were suffused with exquisite odors that rose up around me like a mist. On cool autumn mornings, in the backyard of my family's house, I would sit cross-legged in a huge pile of damp oak leaves, red and yellow and spotted with black, their weightless bulk shifting over me as the wind blew them in whorls of color . . . but it was the pungent, mouthwatering odor of decay that I couldn't get enough of, that I inhaled deeply, and that transported me. Once I was in it, I never wanted to leave that place, where everything disappeared but the colors and the smells, and I would have sat there all morning. But gradually my senses grew accustomed to it and it began to recede, and though I tried to hold it, the way you might try to capture a delicate flavor, it grew more and more evanescent, until everything seemed ordinary again, and there I would be, sitting in a pile of wet, dead leaves, feeling a little dizzy and getting cold.

That fleeting feeling was magic for me. I spent a good part of my life in pursuit of it, looking for it in the books I read and in the entertainment I chose and some of the work I did. And when I recognized it in Keith—I mean when I recognized that that deep, comfortable feeling came easily to him—he felt like home.

I loved to watch him work. He was utterly, exquisitely meticulous. Even when he was doing something as straightforward as a mechanical, the way he laid the type—the precision—was beautiful to see. His designs were graceful, distinguished. As his work began winning awards, I was struck by how little it seemed to mean to Keith to have outside recognition. He was indifferent to it. "The recognition's not important," he told me. "It just helps me to get more work."

He saw things differently than I did, and ultimately, he reminded me *how* to see. The way I might read something and be aware of the rhythm of the writing and the texture, he saw rhythms and textures in paintings and design. His wide appreciation of things—of paintings, of old Eastern and Western prints, of all kinds of objects—invited my interest. I began to be able to see almost as if I were stoned, when ordinary things look infinitely fascinating and alive.

And though his refusal to make and enjoy small talk was sometimes a hardship, there was something in Keith's quietness that calmed me. I worked all day in a business in which everyone had something to say and lived to share it, in which the telling of a story was everything. Though I enjoyed participating in that community, I also loved coming home to someone who wasn't competing for my ear. He only spoke to me when he had something to say, and he had a way of cutting right to the point of any issue that seemed to both simplify and elucidate. He seemed to completely lack the capacity to be dishonest.

As much as his quietness sometimes left me feeling excluded in the beginning of our relationship, it was also a sanctuary, and I knew that there was, in Keith's silence, room for me, if we could find a way to join one another there.

3

"I said, 'You poor bastard, you poor bastard,' as I looked at him," Keith told me years later, when we talked about how he felt on the day Brian died. "I was alone with him—with his body—in this room; he was covered with a sheet and I pulled it back so I could see what he looked like. My first thought when I saw his face was, he's so beautiful, so peaceful—his face was unmarked, except for a spot of blood. The back of his head was all bashed in, you know, but I couldn't see that, and when I pulled the sheet back to see his body, there was a big lump on one side where his ribs had been pushed forward. He was hit from the back, I think."

Keith spoke very slowly; I felt as if he were testing each word before he spoke it, testing to see if it would hold the weight of his feelings, or if he would fall through into a drenching sadness. It was hard for me to sit with him and not tell him to stop.

"I wanted to touch him, but I didn't," he said.

"But . . . what did you feel?" I asked him.

Keith was still, remembering. I thought I could see his heart beating through his ivory shirt.

"What did I feel?" he said, finally. He turned to face me, surprised at the memory. A tear sliced a transparent streak down one cheek. "Nothing," he said. "I felt nothing."

Keith said he had to stop at Brian's apartment, not far from the hospital, before we drove back into the city; he needed to find something. With a fierce, desperate energy, he took the two flights of rickety stairs three at a time up to Brian's back door, broke its glass window, and let himself in. I watched from inside the car, where the warm, stuffy air settled over me like a blanket, inducing a welcome lethargy. Reid slept in his car seat in the back, his fat cheeks pink from the heat. Around his temples, his silky hair was damp. I climbed into the backseat, where, with my nose just a couple of inches from his head, I closed my eyes and caught the gentle baby vapor lifting off him in his sleep. I sat there awhile, inhaling Reid's undiluted milky freshness, appreciating its familiarity, the huge love and calm it evoked in me.

Finally, thinking of Keith and needing to stretch, I got out of the car.

Brian had lived in a working-class neighborhood in a rural part of New Jersey. I knew the area, since one of my favorite aunts lived in the prosperous section of the same town, but I had never been on these narrow backstreets, where dogs, running free, nosed around aimlessly in the wild grass that sprouted along the uneven sidewalks and the wood-frame two-story houses seemed to be listing in the dry, still, high-summer heat. There didn't appear to be anyone around, and there was something ghostly about the blank windows of the houses, the vacant yards scattered with overturned riding toys, as if the neighborhood had been suddenly evacuated. Some vague threat lingered on the empty street.

With one eye on Reid, still sleeping in the back of the car, I climbed the steps to Brian's door. I could see that it was dark and cooler inside the house. "Keith?" I called.

"Just a minute," I heard him say, but stepping into the doorway I saw him crouched in the kitchen, rummaging through the contents of a large garbage bag. It was messy and I had the thought—nauseating—that he had gone mad. "Keith! What are you doing? What are you looking for?"

His hair had fallen into his eyes. He turned his head just enough so that he could see me without taking his hands out of the bag. He had the protective, feral look of an animal interrupted at a meal.

"I need to find his works," he said.

I don't remember what of Brian's things Keith carried in a black trash bag back home with us, besides his sneakers and a T-shirt, still soaked with blood and sweat, and a tan spiral-bound notebook he'd found, a kind of diary Brian had kept. But the bag was big and awkward and nearly full and I remember thinking, as Keith lugged it down the stairs to the car, that it looked just as if he were taking out the garbage, and how sad that made me, that inside that clumsy plastic was all Keith had of his brother's things. He had collected the evidence of Brian's addiction, knowing how hard Brian had tried to hide it.

It had gotten dark, and started to rain, and Keith had asked me to drive. I thought he would try to sleep. But when we had been driving awhile, and I looked over at him, thinking, because he was so quiet, that he had nodded off, his face, in the sorry yellow glow of the highway lights, was wet.

"Oh, Keith," I said. I put my hand over one of his.

I was prepared for him to take my hand and hold it tight; to cry. But instead he pulled on me so hard, the car swerved into the next lane. I gasped. There was a long, angry blast from the pickup I had nearly cut off. Keith's grief—a sudden, furious eruption—seemed to expand and fill the car.

"Why? Why?" he shouted above the noise. The baby woke up and started to cry. Keith dropped my arm and pounded the car door with his fist. "Why did he do it?"

Hunching over in the front seat, he sobbed into his hands. Reid wailed from the back.

"It's okay, baby, it's okay," I said, not really knowing who I was talking to. Reid had found his bottle of juice and began to suck himself back to sleep; Keith was crying quietly. I leaned forward to try to see the road. The rain was coming down heavy and fast; the sky ahead went rosy with lightning, then black again. *I can hardly see where I'm going,* I remember thinking, *and it looks like I'm driving right into a fucking storm.*

Keith doesn't remember today who of his family he telephoned to break the news about Brian. He did actually call his sister, who with other members of the family made the arrangements for Brian's wake and funeral. Over the next couple of days, Keith became quieter and more detached as he went about his work at the studio. I was detached, as well. Though I was aware of the drama of what had happened—when I dropped the bomb, Keith's twin brother committed suicide, I expected the shocked, quick intake of breath, the widened eyes, and the hands flying protectively to the faces of my family and friends—I was nowhere near understanding the implications of it. "How awful it must be for Keith," my mother lamented, and I could only think, it must be, because I didn't know. Some of my friends phoned him to tell him how badly they felt for him, or wrote him sympathetic notes. He was polite. Then to me he said, "They don't understand what the fuck they're talking about." But he filed the notes away carefully, knowing, I think, that a time would come when he might appreciate them.

I had never been to a wake. Brian's casket, a framed photograph laid across it, the stands of flowers on either side, gave the odd impression that he had won a race ("And they're off, ladies and gentlemen, Keith and Brian, neck and neck, in a race to their death . . . and the winner is . . . !)

We had left Reid with a sitter, so it was just Keith and me who were wandering among his relatives and Brian's friends and students. For ten years Brian had taught high school English and had been the school's distance and cross-country running coach. One after another the kids shyly approached Keith's father and stepmother, his sister, his aunt, each other. But not one of them spoke to Keith. He stood alone, forlorn and uncomfortable on the shores of grief, while small waves of mourners lapped against his relatives, cooling the heat of their misery.

He wore a pitiful little smile, to say that he was approach-able, to say, *Please come and talk to me, I'm not dead.*

"Why won't anyone speak to me?" Keith whispered as the tide of guests moved further and further from him.

He got his answer from a small, nervous student, who stood watching him for a few moments and then picked his way over to us hesitantly.

"Nobody can look at you, man," said this boy, sweating in his good suit. "It's the picture. You—it's like Brian walking around at his own wake, you know what I mean?"

Keith and I stared at him.

"I mean, Brian's gone, right?" said the boy. He gestured at Keith. "Then, like, how can he still be *here?*"

I think it was from that moment that Keith began to feel like the dead among the living, a pariah, a role he accepted with frightening defenselessness.

"I don't know," he said quietly, submissively. I took his hand, damp and limp inside of mine, and I knew he would be lost.

At first I felt ashamed about how excitedly I had looked forward to meeting Keith's twin brother. Ashamed, because a lot of my excitement was fueled by a sexual energy I didn't want to acknowledge. From the moment I first met Keith, several years before we became lovers, my attraction to him was nourished partly by the quality of intensity in his quietness and partly by my own need to charm him out of that and into life. But after we had lived together for a couple of months, and he remained stuck in the template I had constructed for him, I had begun to become impatient with his silent intensity and my role as charmer. The idea of another Keith, a twin, the same, but different, still mysterious and unknown, held interesting possibilities. Would they look exactly alike? Would Brian have Keith's square jaw and strong chin? Would they act alike? Would I be able to tell them apart? If Brian and Keith had the same eyes, who would I see when I looked into them?

I met Brian on the first Thanksgiving Keith and I spent together, at their grandmother's house, not far from ours. It was the first time I was meeting any of his family, so there was some of that dread you feel when you have to contend with the people who, by their very presence, accentuate the superficiality, the brassy luster of a new relationship, when you most don't want to see it that way.

"Oh, Brian's here already," Keith said happily as we turned into the driveway and pulled up behind a rusted truck with Jersey plates.

I wore a tailored wool suit with a fitted jacket and straight skirt; I wanted to look sexy, but I didn't want to seem to be trying. Walking up the porch stairs to the large, ramshackle house, I suddenly grabbed Keith's arm.

"Remind me," I said. "Why are we doing this?"

"What, Thanksgiving dinner? Okay, the Indians had a

plentiful harvest, and they wanted to share it with the Pilgrims, so . . ."

"Out here, with your family."

"I thought you wanted to meet my family," Keith said. We had stopped at the top of the stairs. Keith pulled me gently toward the house. Partly as a result of my own preoccupation about Brian, and partly because sex was such a comely aspect of my relationship with Keith, I couldn't get away from the idea that all his relatives would see when they looked at us, on a wide screen in living color playing across their collective mind, was what we did in bed.

Keith kissed me lightly on the lips. I closed every button on my jacket and took a deep breath. "Okay, here goes," I said. I stepped aside while Keith opened the door.

We walked into a haze of delicious smells, of roasting turkey and sweet potatoes, steaming vegetables and fruit pies. "Keith's here!" a female voice cried, and then a stream of family collected around us. While Keith embraced his aunt, his cousins, and then his stepmother, his father greeted me warmly and offered to take my coat. As I thanked him and turned to look into the living room, I saw Brian standing half behind a chair. He was more casually dressed than the rest of us; his brown cotton shirt, open-necked, with the sleeves rolled up, dark corduroy jeans, and heavy boots made him look almost as if he'd just walked out of the woods. His arms were folded across his chest, both thumbs tucked under his armpits, and he held his head cocked back a bit, as if someone had a finger under his chin. I broke off from the group and approached him. "Hi," I said, putting out my hand. "I'm Val." When he took my hand, all of his watchfulness fell away. He smiled at me shyly, but unguardedly, and I saw that one of his front teeth just minutely overlapped another, in a way that Keith's did not.

There was no question about being able to tell them apart. Even if I hadn't known one of them well, it wouldn't have been hard. Though their hair was just the same reddish brown color, Keith's was long, which encouraged his habit of running his hand through it to keep it off his face. On Brian, whose short haircut revealed his face in a way that would have seemed too bold for Keith, this gesture would have seemed effeminate, or impatient. Keith, who worked indoors at a drafting table all day, was pale, slender, had the misleading look of a person who is retreating. But Brian, who by then had quit teaching and started a lumber business, and spent a good part of his time cutting down trees and clearing land in the lush and sturdy gardens of northwest New Jersey, was more robust, a bit broader than Keith, and exuded energy and a point of view. This also was misleading. He was cocky, physically, comfortable with his body in a way that Keith was not, but he shared Keith's courteous, gentle, almost tentative demeanor with me. I found this combination enormously attractive and threatening, because it awakened that sexual curiosity and excitement I had imagined before I met Brian. His power was different from Keith's, less ephemeral, more base, more animalistic, more physical. It made me a little afraid to know him.

To me the looks of the two men perfectly reflected their professions: Brian spent his time splitting logs; Keith spent his, metaphorically, splitting hairs.

Yet, as the afternoon at their grandmother's wore on, and I talked with Brian, or watched him talking with his relatives, he and Keith slowly took on an increasing resemblance, which I think was hidden from me originally by the surprise of their differences, as well as my reluctance to look closely at either of them while we were in the midst of their family. But as we sat at the dinner table I realized, looking at Brian's hands lying comfortably on either side of his plate, that they were absolutely indistinguishable from Keith's. Individually, in fact, each of their features was indistinguishable; they began to look like two different composites of the same body. Some moments it seemed as if Brian were a stranger impersonating Keith—not very successfully, but with enough similarity to give me the uncomfortable feeling that I was experiencing a kind of persistent, visual echo. There was something bizarre, undeniably freaky, seeing them standing next to each other, like the feeling you might get looking into a mirror and seeing a reflection that was not quite yourself.

I had already begun to feel as if Keith were the real thing, and Brian an imitation. In fact, it seemed to me that Brian was trying to be a lesser version of his brother.

Since Brian was born five minutes after Keith, I always imagined that he was *the other one.* The boys' births, difficult, came six weeks ahead of schedule: first Keith, slippery and small, barely five pounds. "A boy," I imagined the doctor saying, handing the infant quickly to a nurse. And then, with a tired sigh, "Here comes the other one."

Though I saw Brian intermittently from the time I first met him till his death four years later, I never really knew him. We had both studied to be English teachers; he must have read a lot, or at least a lot of the same books I'd read. Yet we never discussed what had drawn us to literature or to the idea of teaching. I didn't know who his friends were, or if, in fact, he had any friends. Whenever I saw him, he was kind and considerate and polite, but we never talked about anything personal.

One summer, he offered to install air conditioners in the loft. It was a big, difficult job, two or three days of sweltering work, and it was the only occasion I can recall seeing Brian and Keith together for days at a time. Brian chopped neat squares in the brick walls, wrapped a rope around himself, and hung on the outside of the building below the windows as he and Keith fitted the heavy appliances in. I was sure he would fall and kill himself, but he seemed unconcerned. He was all business. We had moved what little furniture we had out of the living room, and Brian had brought in a big old creaky wheelbarrow to mix cement in, and set it right in the middle of the floor. I watched as he and Keith moved fluidly behind a scrim of pale sunlight, while cement dust swirled around them like smoke. The two of them looked so different: one, shirtless, substantial, and muscular in shorts and construction boots; the other, slight, in a baggy fifties-style short-sleeved shirt and lightweight dungarees that made him seem to have shrunk into his clothes. They worked together easily, without speaking much. "Here," one would say mildly to the other, passing a tool or handing over some tape or tubing. "Right. Here," the other would say, passing something back. It seemed to me as if they had done this same job a million times before, both knowing instinctively what came next, who did what, and how.

"Well, that wasn't too bad, was it?" Brian said after it was over. He popped a couple of beers, took a long, noisy swig from one of them, and with his palm rolled the cold bottle across his forehead.

Keith poured his into a glass. "Coulda been worse," he said, "you hanging out the window." He waited till the foam sank a bit before he drank.

They stood there in the kitchen looking at each other a minute and then laughed their identical laugh.

I never completely got over the freak-show aspect of seeing them together. When, months later, Keith and Brian's identical-twin first cousins showed up at their grandmother's for a holiday dinner—men about the same age as Keith and Brian, and to me, much more seriously indistinguishable—I couldn't help gawking at the oddity of their family's prominent genetic stutter. The family was accustomed to it, of course, the sight of two sets of twins at the holiday table. But the double-twinning made their congregation seem weird and fascinating, as if they belonged to some deviant subculture. I think that this idea—that they were a peculiar family—somehow made both Keith and Brian's later behavior acceptable to me.

4

More than once, he dreamed his brother's death.

Just after we'd been married, I woke up one morning to see Keith sitting on the side of the bed in the gray half-light of dawn. I sat up, too, quickly, partly to see him better, partly because I was frightened. Sleep, to me, has always been welcoming, and waking from it I feel that I am leaving a place of warm, delicious seclusion, protected and strengthened by rest and dreams. I was bewildered by people for whom sleep is not an ally. The first couple of times I awoke to find Keith gone from our bed in the middle of the night, I assumed he was up because he wanted to be, not that sleep was eluding him, or wickedly offering him the dreadful alternative of his dreams. But often he couldn't sleep, he told me; his mind was full of energy, clattering with ideas. When he did fall asleep, overcome by exhaustion, he had vivid nightmares. This morning, three years before Brian died, he had had a recurring one.

"I had that dream again that Brian was killed," he said. When I touched his arm, his skin was damp and cold. "His motorcycle went off the road."

I saw then that he had been crying.

After Keith and I had been living together for a couple of months, Brian drove in on his motorcycle to visit us for the first time at home. He wore a black leather jacket and pants, black leather gloves, and a sleek-looking black helmet. As usual for him, he was late; his unpredictability was frustrating for both Keith and me. I had given up on seeing him and gone to bed, but

Keith waited, wanting to see him, and pretty sure that he would show up.

I was reading in bed, around midnight, when Brian finally came. I could hear him in the hall as Keith greeted him and he made an excuse about why he was late. Then I heard my name, and their footsteps, Brian's heavy in his motorcycle boots, as they approached the bedroom. I was naked under the sheets and pulled them up reflexively when both men entered the room. The cold air clung to Brian's clothes as if it had accumulated on him during the ride; now, inside the warm house, it emanated from him with a sharp, metallic smell. He had removed his helmet and, holding it under one arm, extended his other hand, in the coarse, black glove, toward me. He touched my bare shoulder with his index finger. "Hi, Val." I laughed. Brian teased me about not waiting up for guests, and I said something about needing to get enough sleep, while Keith stood off to one side, arms folded, and watched. I had a fleeting thought about what it would be like to have both brothers in bed with me. After a few minutes more of conversation, Keith kissed me good-night and put his arm loosely around Brian to guide him out of the room. As I drifted off to sleep, their muffled talking in the living room sounded like one voice. When one of them sharply burst into laughter, I could not tell which man it was.

"I wonder what Brian was thinking, seeing you against those pink sheets last night," Keith said casually the next day. He seemed amused. Though the tension in the room had been undeniable, and not unpleasant, Keith's remark gave me the willies. I felt as if Keith had been showing me off, showing his brother up. In all the time I knew him, I never lost the feeling that by being Keith's wife, I was hurting Brian in some subtle way.

Keith's father, a salesman when the boys were babies, quickly climbed the corporate ladder till, by the time the boys were six years old, he was running his large company's entire Canadian operations. The family lived in northern New Jersey until the twins were four, and another baby—a girl—was born. Then Jim was transferred to Montreal. There they owned a boat and motored in it on the St. Lawrence, and skiied often. But neither of the boys developed close friendships; when they moved back down to New Jersey more than ten years later, there were no deep ties to break for either of them. "The twins never seemed to have much fun when they were kids," their sister, Maggie, told me. "They didn't have a lot of friends, and they seemed to take everything very seriously.

"Even normal things that kids do, they did to an extreme," Maggie recalled. "Brian had an insect collection. You should have seen it; it could've been in the goddam Smithsonian.

"They were totally disciplined, straight-A students. Brian was a track star, Keith an expert skiier. But if they weren't studying, they were practicing their sports. They hardly dated; I don't think Brian even had a date till after he left for college.

"Something about my brothers always made me sad," Maggie said.

Brian's girlfriend, a remarkably talkative telephone line maintenance worker, accentuated and enlarged my discomfort around him. Her manner was tough and ruffian, and she was aggressive about trying to get to know us, as if friendship were a jar with a stuck lid that needed to be whapped at with the dull side of a knife in order to be gotten into. She dressed almost exactly as Brian did, in jeans and plaid shirts and sturdy brown round-toed boots—so that she struck me more as his *teammate* than his girlfriend. Or rather, a member of the opposing team. The way she punched Brian in the arm to get him to respond to something she'd said, or swatted him nonchalantly with the back of her hand if she didn't like his response, made me wonder at their relationship. What did they do together? Play football?

On an evening Evalyn and Brian had come in for dinner at our house, she grabbed the corkscrew I was about to use and waved it in Brian's direction. "Hey, kinda looks like one of those sexual aids we'd like to try, doesn't it, Bri?" she said, glancing at Keith and me sideways. As I watched her getting ready to leave that night, the flat, gray fur on the collar of her bolero jacket reminded me of roadkill. "We have to do this again," she said happily as they were waiting for the elevator.

"Yes, we have to," I said.

She seemed to increase Brian's vulnerability around us. And at the same time, made it more difficult to talk to him.

One Easter Sunday, at a family dinner, Evalyn pleasantly asked where my mother lived.

"Fair Lawn," I told her.

"Fair Lawn?" she exclaimed, as if I had said Perth Amboy or Port Newark or some other notoriously degenerate New Jersey town. "Why would she live there? It's full of Jews!"

"Must be why she lives there," I said flatly, glancing at Keith and taking another mouthful of food. It took a moment before my response sank in.

It was easy, of course, not to feel sorry for her, caught waving her prejudices mindlessly around the dinner table, but for Brian, who would not look at me, I felt sad. "Do you feel the way she does about Jews," I wanted to ask, "or anyone? Do you really?"

I wanted to take him over to our side, to take care of him, to show him that he deserved better than what he allowed himself, but I didn't know how to do that, and besides it seemed (and would have been) presumptuous. Instead, I began to feel self-righteous, and naturally wanted to avoid situations where we'd be seeing Brian with Evalyn, who, in an effort to show what an unbiased good sport she really was, followed me around the living room after dinner that Easter Sunday, deeply interested in whatever I happened to be saying, or asking me irritating questions like, "How can you live in New York City?" *Easy,* I wanted to say, *it's full of Jews.*

5

When Keith and I decided to be married—or, I should say, when I decided that Keith and I should be married—I don't remember much enthusiasm on Brian's part. I wanted him to be excited, to be happy for his brother. To be fair, I have to say that Keith wasn't especially enthusiastic either, at first. We had been living together for a couple of years and I had the idea that if Keith wouldn't marry me, it meant that we were in some kind of stasis. This was true, but I didn't understand that sending the shock of marriage through a stagnant relationship wasn't necessarily going to jolt us into anything; it would just jolt us, after which I would slowly sink to the bottom of a sea of ambivalence while holding fast to the heavy weight of my commitment. But at the time, "Marry me or else" was my ungentle proposal, the "else" being packing up my gear and trolling the waters for less reluctant fish. That prospect was unpleasant for me, and must have been for Keith, too, because after eyeing the bait reluctantly for a couple of weeks, he swallowed it. ("I was afraid that if I didn't marry you, I'd lose you," Keith told me later. "I wasn't ready to get married again, but I wanted you.") Suddenly I was the one who felt squirmy, realizing that it was not only Keith, but me as well, who'd gotten hooked. I wanted to get married because it seemed like the next step in our relationship; I needed proof that for me as well as Keith, we were in an alliance that would last . . . for a while, anyway. I didn't want to marry him because I was madly in love with him and wanted to spend the rest of my life with him. I didn't really know what I wanted to do with the rest of my life. But I was afraid of getting older—I was over thirty—and I knew that I wanted a child, and Keith seemed like a good bet in the husband/father department. That is, I thought I could get what I needed from him. I felt superior to him, in a way, more sophisticated; his world was very circumscribed. There had been his marriage, and his work. Now there was me. I would show him how to have fun. Whatever there was about him that didn't suit my idea of who my husband would be, I would fix.

As a way of downplaying the importance of what we'd decided (or what I'd felt I'd pushed Keith into), I began taking the idea of getting married only half seriously. It never occurred to either one of us to discuss what marriage meant to us; I think we were too scared to admit to each other what on some level we'd already admitted to ourselves: we didn't really know what we were doing. But we went ahead and made plans, anyway, arranging a small wedding ceremony in a judge's chambers, and inviting my mother and younger sister and Brian to be our witnesses. For a party the next night, the rest of our families were coming in.

The afternoon of our wedding, my mother and then-unmarried sister, both blooming with anticipation in soft, floral-printed dresses, settled prettily among the rubble of our loft—then in its most primitive state of renovation—while Keith and I put on serious clothes, formal enough for the business we were about to undertake. It was a beautiful, hazy, warm May afternoon, the kind of afternoon that makes you feel as if one thing will flow easily into another, and I remember thinking at some point that that wasn't the way it was going to be. We needed two witnesses for our marriage, and though we'd decided on my mother and Brian, representing both of our families, I had asked my sister to come along, too. As the time approached for us to leave for city hall, and Brian had not yet shown up, I remembered having had the thought that it was a good thing I'd asked my sister in case Brian didn't come. Feeling mean-spirited about assuming irresponsibility on Brian's part, I hadn't wanted to acknowledge the idea. But as it became clear that Brian was not going to make it, I felt both angry and sad. Keith would be married without anyone from his family looking on. As we were about to leave the house, Brian phoned. His truck had broken down, he had to have it towed; he'd try to come in time for dinner after the ceremony. Though Keith showed no disappointment, I wanted to console him. "I'm sorry about Brian," I said in the back of the car on our way downtown.

"It figures," Keith said. He shrugged, as if to cast something off. "It's all right." He plucked at something on his trouser leg and glanced out the car window, but then he felt me looking at him, and he turned to me and smiled. He cupped his hand over my knee, and leaned over to kiss me. It wasn't all right, but Keith didn't want it to cast a pall over the afternoon; he wanted to protect us both from his disappointment.

The judge surprised us with a poem after she'd married us, something about rain falling and our keeping each other from getting too wet (or maybe it was about dancing together in the rain and getting very wet), and out of nervousness and happiness and the poem's absurdity, I got a nearly uncontrollable case of giggles. Also, the judge, though attractive, had a cross-eye, which I only noticed toward the end of the ceremony when I tried to look at her before I said, "I do."

Keith wore no ring. Mine, which had been my mother's, was too large for my fourth finger; rather than have it sized, I wore it on the third finger of my left hand, where it did not look like a wedding band. That was just fine with me. Maybe one day when I felt sure that Keith and I were really a good fit, I would have the ring adjusted. It was an apt symbol for what I was unable to acknowledge: the whole idea of marriage, the expectation circumscribed and burnished in my mind to an unattainable perfection, was simply too big for me.

When Brian finally arrived, just before dinner, he seemed pissed off. The problem with his truck had turned into some kind of fiasco, I think, or maybe he was just anticipating our being angry and wanted to head it off. But sometime during that evening and the next evening's party, he began to enjoy himself. He and my sister noticed each other.

I watched them out of the corner of my eye as they danced, first every couple of dances, and then every one. They stared, uninhibited by what we or our friends would think, as if they'd never seen anything like one another before. The energy between them seemed to build precipitously. Later that night, as Keith and I lay in bed, barely touching, my happiness, ground down and dampened by cocaine and alcohol, turned gritty: I had just gotten married and I didn't know why. Some distant murmuring made me open my eyes.

Brian and my sister, in the next room, trying to quiet their desire, were smoothly consummating our marriage.

The next morning, my sister, still wearing the flowered dress of the night before, her blond curls uncombed, tendriled, and wild around her shoulders, stood framed in one of the large windows of our house. Brian came up behind her quietly, and laid the flat of his hand on her lower back. It was a tender gesture, and careful. He said something to her I could not hear, and she turned to him for a moment with a serious look. "I think I'll go home myself," I thought I heard her say. They drew apart slowly, and as my sister went to get her bag and say good-bye to Keith, Brian turned sort of aimlessly back to the window. Shortly after that weekend, my sister settled out West. She and Brian never saw each other again.

"He was so sensitive," my sister said about Brian a couple of years ago. "He seemed concerned about me. You know, I really, really liked him." She sighed. "But I need to apologize to you." She had phoned me for this reason, explicitly. It was nearly a decade since that night, but she and I had not spoken about it before. "I was envious of you," my sister continued. "I think I used Brian as a way to get a taste of what you and Keith seemed to have. I've felt bad about it all this time."

I knew it all along, of course, that they were that night, in the jumbled dialect of our celebration, a kind of declension of bride and groom. Maybe this was why I had felt so matter-of-fact about their behavior. No matter how hard I tried to get a comfortable grip on my sister's carefully shaped apology and hold it to me, I could not. As I tried to explain this to her, I began to feel sorry about both her and Brian, wondering whether during their short connection, each was for the other only an apology for Keith and me.

"Please forgive yourself," I begged my sister. "I just want you to be able to forgive yourself." As soon as I said it, an image of Brian's face, vivid, warm with the high-coloring of life, swam up before my closed eyes. The vulnerability of his expression was so acute that it moved something physical in me; I made a small, gasping "oh!" sound. "What is it?" my sister asked.

How much I wanted to be able to say that to Brian, too.

Keith's father and stepmother lent us their condo on Hilton Head for a long weekend soon after we were married. It was one of the few times Keith and I had flown anywhere together, and I felt excited, alert to the experience. No matter how often I fly and how blasé I start out, inevitably I look out of one of those small scratched patches of plastic onto the woolly roots of clouds and I think: this is a miracle of imagination, being up here on the underside of the sky. It is *people* who have imagined this, and made it real. Then the unnaturalness of this reality, the gall of assuming a relaxed posture inside of a large piece of machinery hurtling through the air, makes me feel humble and queasy. It is the plain, solid, and uncomplicated dry-toast quality of trust that settles me down.

I noticed instantly after we boarded the plane at La Guardia that one of the stewardesses looked at Keith with a peculiar familiarity. Well, I guess he is kind of handsome, I thought, narrowing my eyes in a shifty appraisal, trying to imagine I was seeing him again for the very first time. Having had the experience that familiarity often breeds familiarity, I thought maybe she was flirting. From afar. I filed it.

But no. Now, as we settled into our seats, she stood in the aisle and stared at him with a boldness and a kind of knowing smile that implied a secret, shared knowledge. "Don't I know you?" she asked Keith.

He looked back at her, barely. "No, sorry."

As she moved up and down the aisle, chatting with passengers and preparing for takeoff, she continued to glance back at Keith curiously.

"Do you know her?" I asked him. Then, conspiratorially, as if we were spies working for the same side, I said, "It's okay, you can be straight with me."

Keith looked up blankly from his magazine and then turned to me. "What are you talking about?" he said. "I never saw her before. She's just weird."

"Two orange juices," the stewardess said, putting mine down first. As she carefully leaned past me to give Keith his, she said with certitude, "You came for me on your motorcycle on a blind date two years ago. You don't remember me? You don't remember that night?"

"She thinks you're Brian," I said aloud, not to explain, but needing to tie a knot on the end of that morning's string of small resentments.

"My brother," said Keith. "You went out with my twin brother." If Brian was struggling, we didn't know it, and we felt generous about our confusion, and enjoyed the stewardess's amazement.

6

Though our marriage might have seemed healthy, even this early on I knew that it was troubled. Whenever I wanted affection, Keith seemed preoccupied; whenever he wanted affection, I seemed to be taking something out of the oven. "What is it?" I finally cried at him in exasperation. "You like me in oven mitts?" He turned away, sulking.

What I initially responded to in Keith was his distance, his remoteness. I wanted to be the one who brought him into the present, the beacon who guided him back from that dark, silent place he went to. I didn't understand when I met him that that role I had chosen for myself was a reiteration of the role I wished I had been able to succeed at with my father: to get him to share his sad secret with me. The problem was, simply, that the task with Keith (as it would have been with my father) was impossible. Keith's distance and his silence only grew wider and deeper the more I tried to reel him in.

My father's grief was the secret in our family. I knew a few morbid facts: that his mother had died when he was thirteen, and an uncle—his mother's brother—had sued for custody of my father, and won. My father didn't see his father again until he was an adult. My grandfather (whose name was never spoken in our family) had lurked around the lobby of the building where my dad worked as a reporter for United Press just to be able to get a glimpse of him. At my grandfather's funeral, there was a murmur of disapproval from his family, from whom my father had also been estranged, when my father stepped forward to say the Kaddish. "Shall I say it with you?" asked the rabbi.

"No," my father said, "I'll say it myself."

The pain this rupture in my father's life caused him was

apparent to all of us children—my older brother, my sister, and me—but he never spoke about it. Though my mother remembers my father's sadness and his courage at my grandfather's funeral, she doesn't know either the full story of why my father was taken from him as a child or how he felt about it. When my father died suddenly over ten years ago, the possibility of ever knowing was closed.

I try to piece together a mosaic of who he was, how his life before me shaped him, and consequently the father he was to me. Choosing from among many shards of richly colored memories, I can easily construct the shimmering pattern I recognize as Dad. But stepping back from childhood into the perspective of adulthood, when I try to see him as a man separate from what I can remember of my own experience of him, the color drains away, the mosaic turns transparent, the pattern disappears. I never knew him.

My father's secret had become a warning for me: there are some things too difficult to talk about. But how could he not have understood that in trying to protect himself and his family from his pain, he was protecting his pain instead, isolating it, keeping it safely uncontaminated by understanding and consolation? He made it his alone, and it gave him a formidable power.

That secret, sharpened by our intimidation, was the fulcrum of my family's delicate emotional equilibrium. As much as my mother loved my father, as much as we children adored him, we never required him to share that part of himself with us, even though it affected all of our relationships with him and with each other. (And, later, with our own husbands and wives and our children.) Never wanting to tip him over the edge into anger or depression, we were careful around him. I think now of what our fear cost us and I refuse to repeat that experience with Keith.

Soon after we were married, Keith's silences began to move in on our relationship like a fog. The quality of his quietness seemed to change; when I first met him, I thought I could see him behind his silences. Now he seemed to disappear into them.

The problem became particularly acute for me during dinnertime, when I would want to be sharing the events of my day— I was still working as a magazine editor—and hearing about his. Dinnertimes with my family when I was growing up were a raucous affair, we three kids competing for my father's attention. Whoever told the best story, had the funniest anecdote, was graced with his benevolent mirth. But Keith seemed not to want to talk about what he was thinking, and would often respond to my questions in monosyllables. He seemed untroubled by the shroudlike silence that hung over us, night after night.

When I felt as if all of my attempts to engage him had failed, I decided to try a different tactic. I resorted to holding up little signs I had made out of blue, unlined index cards on Popsicle sticks. One evening, after we had sat down to eat and I had begun to feel irritated by the predictable silence from across the table, I held up one of my signs: HOW WAS YOUR DAY? Keith looked over at me. "Cute," he said. Well, it was a start, anyway. More silence. I held up another: PENNY FOR YOUR THOUGHTS. Keith raised his eyebrows and carefully cut a piece of meat off his lamb chop. I held the sign close to my face and twirled it coquettishly. Keith gave me a weak smile, then let out a sigh. I tried a third one: JESUS IS COMING. No reaction. Keith continued to eat, but my dinner was getting cold. Finally, I pulled out the last. THE END IS NEAR, it said. I held it above my head and stared solemnly at my husband.

When I think back to that time, I remember feeling distraught, angry, frustrated. I tried to talk with Keith about the way I felt, but he didn't seem to understand what the problem was:

"Why does it bother you that we don't talk all the time?" he asked. He felt that I had changed the rules, and in a way, I had. Whereas I had seemed not to mind his silences months ago, now they distressed me. "It's different now," I told him, but I couldn't then explain how. I had thought he would change. I had thought, If you spend enough time with me, I'll make you the guy I want you to be.

It would have been easier to have walked out then, before we had the baby, before the smack of Brian's death sent Keith reeling and left me standing on the shaky, unstable terrain of our marriage, stunned and scared. But even from the beginning of our relationship, when I knew that, due to his reticence and his inner-directedness, Keith would not be an easy man, and then all through the years after Brian's death when it sometimes felt as if there were almost nothing at all between Keith and me but sadness and resentment, one truth remained: I never wanted to leave Keith as much as I wanted to be with him.

It sounds so reductive, put that way. Not anything like my idea of the romantic love I had imagined would blossom in my marriage, sweetening it with devotion. Sometimes I felt afraid to leave, because I was afraid to be alone; but mostly, once we were married, I simply did not want to give up. I kept thinking: there's too much in this man that I love and admire, to walk away from him. He's good in the ways I want to be good; strong in the ways I want to be strong; gentle and generous in the ways I want to be. I knew these qualities were there, even when I had lost sight of them, or when Keith could not reveal them.

And there was something else, some fundamental connection I could not articulate. Maybe it was only a conspiracy in our emotional histories, but I knew that our roots were tangled long before we met.

A year into our marriage, Keith had all but disappeared into his work, or behind the pulverizing pain of the migraine headaches that often felled him and the pills that he took to kill the pain. Almost nothing about our life was what I had thought it would be. Except for when we were making love—which was still often and passionate—Keith almost always seemed irritated; even when things were going smoothly, he seemed to be on the edge.

He watched me one morning as I was showering, watched me with such intentness that I asked him, "What? What are you looking at?"

"You're pregnant," he said. He didn't know that my period was a little late; I hadn't mentioned it because I wasn't suspicious.

"I don't think so," I said, though I felt a thrill. "What makes you say that?"

"I don't know, honey," Keith said, turning away. "It's just a feeling."

He was right. When my period was a week late, then two, I took a pregnancy test. By then, I knew I was pregnant, too, by the swelling in my breasts and the fullness across the lower part of my belly.

The ring at the bottom of the test tube turned blue: positive.

I went out to the front of the loft to get Keith. "Come with me," I said. "I want to show you something." I had never felt so happy or excited. Keith took my hand and walked back with me into the kitchen. I pointed to the blue ring. "We have an embryo," I said.

Keith squeezed my hand as we stared at the test tube. He sighed. "Shit," he said.

"Keith," I said. I turned to face him. "I'm so happy! I'm pregnant!"

"I know, hon," he said. "Wow." He rubbed his temples.

"Do you have a headache?" I asked.

"I don't know."

"Are you happy?"

"I don't know. I guess so."

He caught the streak of pain as it cut across my face. Then, sorry, he took me in his arms and kissed my hair. "I *am* happy, honey," he said. But his uncertainty had penetrated my happiness, had lodged in it like a wick, and all through the pregnancy it fueled a tiny flame of hurt and resentment. He did want to have a baby, he said, but he didn't feel ready; the timing was bad. I understood not feeling ready: how could anyone ever be ready? That was not the point. The point was that we were going to have a baby. The point was to *get* ready.

After the initial surprise, Keith seemed to become accustomed to the idea. For a while, he was more attentive; that summer we spent weekends lazing around a house we had rented in the country, reading, talking, making love. Every Saturday night he took me to a nearby inn where he picked at his dinner while I devoured thick slabs of rare roast beef and a couple of baked potatoes; I felt so extremely feminine in my fertility that I was pleased to be eating like a man. Keith chronicled the pregnancy with photographs he took every couple of weeks of me naked, standing in stark profile against one of the white walls of the loft, or sitting, more softly lit, the light from a window glowing on the smooth, satiny swell of my belly. I took a shot of him with a salad spinner tucked under the belt of his robe and labeled the picture *Keith, 36 weeks.* His expression is identical to mine in the photographs taken during that time. His face says, "Can this really be happening to us?"

The first week in February, three weeks before the baby was due, my water broke. I felt stretched to the bursting point. Early one morning—feeling like a barge in the increasingly narrow slip of our double bed—I tried to maneuver a turn without waking Keith. There was a faint "pop" below deck, a delicate snap just under the hull. Then I began to leak.

I rolled out of bed, put on a pad, called the doctor, and started preparing a list of what I needed to bring to the hospital and what we still needed for the baby. As I was writing, Keith shuffled out of the bedroom. From the painful look on his face I knew he had a migraine.

"What are you doing?" he asked.

"I'm getting ready to go to the doctor. I think I'm going to have the baby. My water broke."

"Oh shit," Keith said.

"A headache?" I said impatiently.

Keith nodded, then pulled a prescription bottle of Fiorinal out of his robe pocket and shook out a couple of pills.

"I'd like you to come with me to the doctor," I said.

"Maybe if I lie down for a bit I'll feel better," said Keith. "Wake me when you're ready to go."

The obstetrician met us at his office before regular office hours, looking sweetly disheveled, his gray hair combed hastily and his jacket buttoned wrong. "Get undressed, hop up on the table, and we'll see what we've got here," he said. He disappeared for a moment while I took off my clothes. I threw my panties playfully over to Keith, who waited, slightly dazed and uncomfortable, by the examining room door. They sailed in a dainty arc and alighted like an open butterfly on the shoulder of his coat. As the doctor returned, he plucked them off and dropped them on a chair with the rest of my clothes.

"Oh, yes, I see, here we are," the doctor said as he examined me. Then, because he suspected that I might have genital herpes, he scheduled me for a cesarean section early that afternoon and insisted that I go straight to the hospital without stopping at home to pack a bag. Keith would drop me off at the hospital, go home to get my things, and then come back.

In a small, cold room on the maternity floor, I was prepped. A white-haired nurse spoke to me kindly: "Get into bed, and soon you'll have your baby." As I sat alone on the bed, I could hear a woman in the next room making a wonderful fuss. She was screaming and swearing as her cot was wheeled out into the hall. Excited by the commotion, envious that I wasn't going to be having the same kind of mind-ripping ride, I peeked out of my room to see. "Where's my husband! Where's my husband!" the woman cried, panting and thrashing. The huge mound of her belly seemed to be jumping spasmodically under the sheet. Fumbling with his glasses, nearly crying himself, her husband grabbed for her as he ran alongside. "Oh, God, oh God, I'm here, baby," he whimpered.

My feet were cold. I had worn nylon socks to the doctor's office and they weren't heavy enough. Also, they were black-and-white-striped, like the socks the witch wore in *The Wizard of Oz,* the unforgettable socks that, under the house that has crashed on her, spookishly shrivel and smoke. I didn't want to have my baby while I was wearing those socks. It didn't feel right. I wanted wool, L.L. Bean socks, woodcutter's socks. Socks that hugged my feet like happy endings.

I had asked Keith to bring me a couple of pairs of argyles along with my other stuff, but he hadn't returned. My delivery was scheduled for two o'clock; it was now after one. I called the studio. No one there had seen him.

Pulling the flimsy hospital robe over my belly, I went over to the window. The East River was gray and choppy, bleak. I shivered as I watched a couple of seagulls drift in the cold wind. Was I going to have the baby alone? What if Keith never showed up? Well, what could I do about it? I took a breath and folded my hands under the hard swell of my stomach as if to support it. I would take care of myself. Suddenly my eyes smarted.

"Hi, I'm back," Keith said from the doorway.

Still facing the window, I wiped my eyes quickly. "Where've you been?"

"I went to get your stuff."

"Keith," I said, facing him, "that was hours ago."

"Well, I couldn't find anything, hon."

The anesthesiologist came up behind him. "Knock, knock," he said, pushing his way into the room. "I'm Dr. Stone. I'm here to make you numb."

"Suction! Suction!" I heard, and then a baby's cry. "You have a son," the doctor said, "a big, healthy boy."

"A boy!" I called to Keith, who was hanging around what was beginning to seem like his customary spot near the door. "We have a boy!" as if it were a new, exotic sex. A nurse held Reid, wrapped in a pale green sheet, above me. I lifted my head to see him better; all that was visible beneath the sheet was his little face, puffy and scrutinizing. *My son!* Under the steel dome of the harsh operating-room lamp we squinted at each other.

"Don't you want to kiss your baby?" asked the nurse. My arms were tied down, spread out on either side of me crucifix-style, as if I were going to be raised up and hung. A doctor, trying to put everything back, was laboring over the deadened lower half of my body. "The colon, it's slipping!" he said urgently; I felt the operating table tilt forward mechanically. "No, no, the other *way!''* he said, and the table moved again. I pictured my colon, black and slimy, coiling in a deadly glide toward my throat. I swallowed hard.

"Oh, right, of course, my baby," I said, focusing on Reid, who hovered facedown above me in the nurse's arms. Straining to reach him, I gave him a peck on the forehead, and the nurse, satisfied, carried him off.

Keith came to visit in the evening, but he hardly spoke; some nights he seemed to be falling asleep in the chair. Though I didn't know it, he was working in the studio nearly around the clock, sometimes till three or four in the morning, crashing for a couple of hours, and then getting up at six. The idea of supporting a family had cast a spell of fear on him; working was the only way he knew how to deal with it.

I was alone most of the day in my hospital room, either dozing or willing the hot wound at the base of my belly—no longer hard, but a soft jiggly jelly-swell of a belly—to heal. Reid stayed in the nursery. I couldn't keep him in the room with me till I was able to get up and move around.

"What's the matter with you?" I'd ask Keith when he'd come to see me. He would rub his head and look away. One night, exasperated, I began to cry. "This is terrible," I said. "I can't talk to you, you won't talk to me, why are you even coming here?"

Keith looked at me angrily. "I don't know," he said. Then, more forcefully, he said, "What do you want from me?"

"I want you to talk to me, to be with me, to be happy with me," I said, sobbing now, and trying to catch my breath. "It feels like you don't want to come here to see me and the baby, and I don't know why." I was sitting on the side of the bed, and I shifted position painfully. "Oh, ouch, goddamit," I said. "Oh, hell."

Keith handed me a tissue. "I'm sorry," he said. His voice was flat and dead. "I'm really sorry, Val. I'm doing the best I can." He picked up his coat and left.

I didn't know then that Keith had been spending time with the baby before he came to see me. The nurses knew him; he gave Reid bottles of water and formula, and took snapshots of him. Every night he held him and rocked him and stared into his perfect face till the nurses came to take his son away.

The morning of the day we had to sign the papers officially naming our son—we had been stalling, and we didn't really know why, because we'd chosen a name—Keith phoned. The oddest thing had happened, he said, and he had to talk to me about it. We had decided to call our son Reid, because I wanted to name him after my father, whose name was Arthur, but who was called Red for his hair. Reid means "red-haired" in Celtic, and it seemed close enough for our brown-haired boy. But just before he awoke this morning, Keith said, he had heard a voice, clear, distinct, say to him, "Aaron. Name him Aaron." It wasn't a name either one of us had even considered.

"*Aaron?*" I asked Keith. "Where'd you get that from? Was it a voice you recognized?"

Keith said no; it seemed as if it were in the room with him, but he had never heard it before. It was like some über-voice, he said. "I don't know, hon, I just feel really strongly about this, like it's something we should do. Can we give him both names?"

I liked the name, so we agreed to use both, but still call our baby Reid.

Later that day, sitting up in the hospital bed, I related the story by phone to my mother. She was silent when I'd finished. "Mom?" I said. "You there?"

"Aaron is the name your grandfather wanted to give your father," she told me, "but your grandmother refused."

7

"I never allowed myself to acknowledge the sadness I felt during the time of Reid's birth," I told Keith one night after I had been thinking about it recently. "I wanted it to be something that we shared, something joyful, but instead I felt almost completely disconnected from you."

"Why are you sad about it now? It's over long ago."

"The events are over, but my feelings are still there. I've never shared them with you; I think doing that is helping me to recover some of what I'd wanted for us. And besides—excuse the psychobabble—I believe the feelings we had then inform the way we feel now."

Keith sat for a moment in silence. I thought about what it took to extract himself from the familiar hum of his work and the predictability of our life to begin to probe the feelings that had lain, like mine, beneath the surface, for years undisturbed. I thought: What a pain in the ass I am. Then, Fuck it; this is important.

"I remember holding Reid," Keith said finally, "and feeling afraid. I had no idea how to be a father, what he would need from me, what I could give to him. Or to you.

"That's why I spent every night after he was born until you came home from the hospital trying to fix up his room. It was the only way I knew how to be useful. Being around you made me feel useless."

"That's so sad," I said, thinking of how I'd wanted it to be instead. Keith held me, kissing me lightly on the top of my head, while I cried.

꿈

Two days after the cesarian I was well enough to get out of bed and walk around. I hadn't yet held Reid, and my breasts felt like two enormous sacks of rock. Because I had been a suspected herpes case (though the cultures turned out to be negative), I wasn't allowed out on the maternity floor, but I was determined to see my baby. I put on my robe and ventured out of the room, taking measured steps—ouch! yikes! ouch! yikes!—and holding my torso at just the right angle so that I wouldn't pull the incision. I had never before had an operation and I was totally unprepared for the aftereffects. Like a child surprised by the burn of a stove, I was ambushed by its immobilizing hurt. When I first tried to move after the anesthesia wore off, the pain in my abdomen seized me sharply and held me to the bed. I lay there taking shallow little breaths and experimenting with which parts of my body I could move without pain: toes, yes. Lift one knee, yes. Arms, yes. Lift head, whoops! I gripped the bed. I might as well have been sewn to the mattress through my navel. Once I got up and began to get around, I could feel the pain lurking wickedly, ready to stick me behind every step. Now, listing a quarter of an inch off in any direction provoked a searing burn—like a hot iron poking my gut—and made me want to yell.

An orderly spotted me in the hall: "You're not supposed to be out here."

"I'm just going to look at the babies," I said pleasantly as I inched along in an ungraceful cesarian stoop. "I'm not going to sit on them."

I leaned gingerly over Reid's bassinet and touched his arm. He lay on his back in the bright light, sleeping deeply. I ran my finger along his arm to his hand. The satin feel of his skin went right to my mouth, and I had to kiss him. Then I kept my face down next to his so that I could breathe his breath. It was warm, incipient. A human spring.

"You can pick him up," said a nurse passing by.

As I cradled him, he stirred and woke, turned his head toward me, and stretched his mouth open wide. One of his eyes was shut, still swollen from birth; he seemed to be giving me a broad, good-natured wink. "All right, Mr. Baby, let's see how this works," I said, opening the top of my robe. He clamped on, my milk flowed, and nothing else mattered in the world.

My mother had driven us home from the hospital and she followed us warily, as I carried Reid, into the house.

"I've fixed up our room, Val," Keith said as he led me down the long hallway to the bedroom. "What do you think?" He had painted the walls white, and had hung a few carefully selected pictures—a delicate Japanese print of a woman reading, with a cat; a serene, woodsy watercolor I'd once admired. And he'd moved the bed, which I noticed was freshly made, so that the room looked both familiar and different. "Do you like it?" he asked.

"Oh, it's great, honey," I said. "It's swell. I like it a lot." Especially the bed. Seeing it, I was suddenly so tired, I felt as if I might fall down.

"Where are you going to put the baby?" my mother asked, glancing out the bedroom door into the unfinished loft.

"I've got his room all ready," Keith said eagerly. "I've been working on it every night. Stayed up till early this morning to finish it."

He led us to the door and opened it. The room was spotless and monk-cell bare. Brown paper completely covered the enormous window. The ceiling had been scraped of old paint, and the exposed pipes were burnished to a matte shine. The wood floor had been finished and it, too, shone with a kind of dull glow in the lightless room. A carved-wood antique cradle sat pitifully in the center of the floor. "Who's sleeping in here," I asked, "little Thomas Aquinas?"

My mother ventured into the room and gave the cradle a tap. As it swung it made a spine-tingling creak.

"It's very nice," she said to Keith. She put her hand on his shoulder. "I can see you worked hard on it."

I rolled my eyes at her.

"What's with the paper curtains?" I said.

"Quit asking so many questions," said Keith, pushing past me gently to leave the room.

"I'm sorry, hon," I said, following him. "It's just that it's kind of . . . spare."

"Well, I thought that few distractions would help him sleep," Keith said.

Reid didn't seem to appreciate the lack of distractions. He never slept more than a couple of hours at a time. One miserable, dark morning toward the end of February, after a night of pretty continuous nursing, I lay in bed, alternately trying to let go of the persistent vision of my nipples exploding into two sharp flames, and then wondering what I was going to do when Reid started crying again. A cold rain, cascading in sheets, slapped heavily against the windows. Keith must have gone quietly off to work during the few minutes I dozed before the phone had woken me up. It was my mother, calling from her winter home in Palm Springs.

"Hi, Val, how are you?"

"I've been up all night," I said tiredly. "My breasts are sore and I'm exhausted and Reid's not sleeping much."

"Where is he now?" asked my mother. "Can I talk to him?"

"He's asleep," I said, irritated that he wasn't screaming so that my mother could hear him. I thought I detected the sound of birds chirping on her end of the line.

"Mom," I said, "this is the nadir of my life."

"Well!" said my mother cheerfully. "Then it can't get any worse, can it?"

Like a mirror reality, invisible, but existing side by side with what we can see, there was another world my husband and his brother had entered that winter when Reid was born, neither of them yet knowing about the other.

Both men were gravitating into a deeper, more dangerous relationship with drugs. Keith had been steadily increasing his intake of Fiorinal, his migraine pill, and within the year would be unsuccessfully trying to fight off a snarling depression that had sunk its teeth into him and wouldn't let go. Brian began shooting cocaine and, despite several attempts to quit, was plummeting fast toward his hard death.

Though one brother dropped off the cliff before the other even saw the end of the road, Keith's and Brian's journeys had each taken a turn along the same treacherous path.

In the photographs we have of Brian taken a year before he died, he looks startlingly healthy and robust. On an afternoon visit along with other members of the family in June or July he relaxed on our sofa in a short-sleeved Adidas shirt and track shorts. In one photograph, he leans on his left elbow against the arm of the sofa, supporting his head, and gazes down at Reid, at four or five months a small, very fat, bald Frodolike creature.

Reid sits comfortably in the crook of Brian's arm, rests one round, padded, dimpled fist on Brian's chest and, pursing his lips, stares with an intense, unbabylike concentration into the camera. Suddenly, in the next photo, Reid's laughing, a wide, toothless, openmouthed belly laugh: the rolling king-sized chuckle of double-chinned chubbyhood.

At Reid's delight, there were shrieks of pleasure and excitement from the twins' sister and aunt. But Brian, unamused, has disengaged from Reid, has moved his arm, the one that cradled Reid, to the back of the sofa, and now sits beside him untouching, legs splayed as if to push himself away from the baby. Is there a trace of impatience on his face? I instantly knew that Brian could not tolerate being so close to the focal point of his family's happiness; he needed to distance himself from the attention. His look says, *What's so great about this baby, anyway? Why were his aunt and sister fawning over him, always wanting to hold him, making such a fuss over him? What was the big deal?*

"That was the afternoon that he asked me what it was like to be a father," Keith told me later. "I didn't answer him. I ignored him."

"But why?" I said.

"I thought the question was absurd."

"What's absurd about wanting to know what it feels like to have a child?"

As Keith thought about it, the look of anger on his face softened to hurt. "I didn't want to answer him," he said, "because I didn't think I *knew* what it felt like to be a father. I loved Reid, but I didn't know how to share myself with him and with you. Also, I felt so displaced; suddenly the attention I had once had all to myself was going to him. And I was afraid to share it."

By the time Reid was a year old, Keith was getting more work than he could handle. He needed to hire more designers and expand his work space. The front third of the loft had gotten too small to house his business comfortably; he decided to rent and renovate a large space nearby.

I shared his excitement as he negotiated with the architects and planned his new studio. But I also noticed that his perfectionism—which I admired and which was obviously one of the elements of his professional successes—was becoming problematic. I knew that everyone who renovated suffered through the torments of contractors and things not going as planned, but for Keith, the problems were intolerable. His headaches seized him more frequently; he began medicating himself with abandon. Because he was so sick and miserable, I found myself afraid to say anything about it, as if pointing out the excess to him would compound his illness. When I did ask him if he thought taking so much medicine was good for him, he told me in the weakest, most resigned way, "I have no choice." It was the only thing that worked, he said; it was the only way he could keep functioning.

I remember seeing him standing by the cabinet in the kitchen where he kept his pills, watching him swallow a couple of Fiorinal, and then some aspirin, and thinking, God, he's taking an awful lot.

It wasn't until months later that I had that thought again, and knew that I had to do something about it.

Throughout the spring before Brian died, and the summer and fall after, Keith had been spending all of his days away from home either overseeing the complicated and endless minutiae of the expansion and renovation of his studio, or on appointments with clients. At least, this was what I thought. In the evenings, when he was late, I had believed what he'd told me: that he was working overtime, or supervising the contractor. Keith had always been intensely involved in his work, as attentive and passionate about it—and as obsessed—as a lover. I expected him to be putting a lot of time into the studio. Because he was absent so frequently, and remote when he was physically present, I turned my attention completely to the baby, and to a book proposal about raising kids I was working on. As obsessed as Keith was with the studio, I was with our child. I was constantly reading about child development and was fascinated by every aspect. Unlike many of my closest friends, who grew bored spending hours tending to their babies, I found it stimulating. Watching Reid stack his plastic cups, red, blue, yellow, and green, his mouth set in utter seriousness and determination, as if he were conducting the most critical experiment, I wondered, what was he learning? What did he understand? I wanted to guide him through the world while I could, help him, encourage him, applaud him. And just when I thought what a fine teacher I was, I was reminded that I was the pupil as often as Reid. One afternoon during a play-date, one of his more rambunctious friends clutched his favorite fire truck and wouldn't give it back. Reid made a pass at it, but the other toddler—a squat, aggressive bruiser, more sumo than child—knocked him down. Reid ran to me, crying, and I took him on my lap. "It's okay, honey," I said, rocking him, "it's okay." Reid pulled away from me and looked at me as if I were nuts. "It's not okay!" he cried.

I believed that raising my son was the most important thing I'd ever do. The work I'd done before Reid was born, the writing, editing, teaching—it was all fun and challenging, but not, for me, profound in the same way.

Though I made some halfhearted noises about wanting

Keith to be around more often, I really did not want him around; it was painful to be with him. He hardly spoke at all, and seemed irritated and restless in the house, like a trapped animal. Actually, I was the one more trapped. I rarely went out without the baby, except for work-related reasons, and I didn't feel comfortable leaving the baby in Keith's care. One morning, when I had slept past seven, I woke up to find Reid playing alone in the living room, near a wide-open window. In the instant before I recognized the potential for danger, I was happy to feel the crisp air on my face, see the intense fall blue of the sky. But as I approached the window I felt a chill; I saw that the baby was not just within crawling distance, but already on a platform that put him parallel with the window ledge. Keith had left the house sometime earlier, thinking Reid was fine, at a year and a half, unsupervised. It didn't occur to him to close the window.

"He could have gotten into anything!" I said later, in a rage that Keith could have been so thoughtless. "He might have fallen out the window!"

"But he didn't fall out the window, did he?" said Keith coolly. "You're always worrying about things that haven't happened." This was true. I *was* worrying about things that hadn't happened—to Reid—and not worrying about what was actually happening—to Keith. I didn't understand then that I was often anxious about our son because I knew that he was *not* safe in Keith's care, but I didn't know that there was good reason that I felt that way. I didn't at that point know that Keith's judgments were not only impaired by depression, but also by drugs. What still astonishes me is how much I accepted; how badly things had to deteriorate before I finally admitted that something was seriously wrong.

When Reid was eight months old, Keith and I took him out West for a visit with my sister and her husband and their new baby. It was the first time we were seeing each other's children,

Keith was very fond of my sister and her husband and, aside from the predictable hassles we had as a result of toting around two babies, the four of us had a lot of fun. We also took a lot of photographs. Going through some of them back home with Keith, we were both struck by how dreadful he looked. Pale, thin, wasted, exhausted. I stared and stared at one picture till I could figure out what it was that disturbed me. "I know what," I said finally. "You look like a drug addict."

"Let me see," Keith said, taking the picture. I thought he might be offended. "You know, you're right," he said. We laughed uneasily.

Why didn't I ask myself then: If he looks like a drug addict, and he acts like a drug addict . . . well, I wonder . . . might he actually *be* a drug addict?

I didn't ask, because I didn't want to know. Anyway, at that point to me a drug addict was someone who sat on a cardboard box in a tenement basement shooting heroin.

I had experimented with drugs since college in the early seventies. My friends and I smoked pot and took hallucinogens. Next decade, when we socialized, we often did cocaine. Two guys I knew got seriously lost on angel dust, but I would never have smoked angel dust, just as I never would have shot any drug into my arm. I took drugs to feel good, or to heighten my senses, so I was suspicious of anything that I believed had the potential, even in modest doses, to hurt me. I was naive and lucky. Before the culture of addiction and recovery became mainstream, I thought addiction was an affliction of a few unfortunates—if I thought about it at all.

Two months after Brian's death, I preferred not to acknowledge the signs that Keith was out of control and spiraling into a crash: his employees telling me with frustration that he was hardly ever available for consultations on jobs, that he seemed completely indifferent to their work and their concerns about clients, that on many days no one at the office knew his whereabouts; that he was often coming home sometime before dawn too wired to sleep. I attributed Keith's behavior both to grief and to excitement about the renovation, but all along, I must have known that there was something terribly amiss, that this man who had been so fanatical about his work, so thoughtful and perfectionistic, so reliable, had begun to resolutely neglect it. I hoped, I guess, that he would pull himself together on his own. For too long, I could not intervene; I think I sensed that when I did, it meant that there was no going back, that he and I and consequently our relationship would change and whatever ideal I had carried around about us and hoped we would one day recover was lost irretrievably. Finally, the prospect of that change became less daunting than what was actually happening.

One morning that fall, my mother stopped by for a visit with me and the baby. I enjoyed being with her in a new way since Reid was born; she was the one person in the world with whom I could be unabashedly adoring of the baby, who shared my awe of him and was unselfconsciously enthusiastic about expressing it. She also represented "family" to me, so it warmed me to have her around, because Reid and I were so often alone, or with couples with children, but rarely with Keith and certainly not a family the way I had always envisioned it.

We were finishing lunch when I heard a commotion at the other end of the loft. Keith had come in; his office manager, a generally soft-spoken and introverted man Keith had known since high school, was with him. I could hear the office manager shouting, but not Keith's response.

"Just a minute, Mom," I said, and got up to see what was going on.

"Where have you been, man?" the office manager shouted, following Keith as he walked away. His red-framed glasses, askew, were slipping down his nose; he pushed them up angrily with the back of his wrist. "I've needed to talk to you for days, I've got clients calling me about jobs and estimates, and I don't know what the fuck to tell them. Goddamit, where have you been?"

"Leave me alone," Keith said quietly. "Make your own decisions. Figure it out for yourself."

"You're wasting studio money! You're destroying the business!"

I could sense that my mother, carrying the baby, was coming up behind me. I watched from the hallway.

"Leave me alone," Keith said again.

All at once, the office manager grabbed Keith by the throat and, in a spasm of fury, put him through the Sheetrock wall. I quickly turned around and shepherded my mother back to the kitchen. She had not seen what had happened, but her eyes were big with fear.

"Jesus, Val, what's going on?" she said. Her hands shook as she put the baby down on the floor.

"I don't know," I said. "Stay here with Reid while I talk to Keith." I ran back to the front.

"Cut it out! Cut it out right now!" I hissed at both men. "You're wrecking the place!" I wedged myself solidly between them.

The office manager left, swearing under his breath. Keith,

looking pathetically passive, sat in the hole his body had made in the Sheetrock.

"God, my head aches," he said.

I helped him out. "Are you all right?"

"I have to lie down for a while," he said. He took a couple of pills before he went into the bedroom and shut the door.

Maybe it was that event that loosened the grip of denial, that gave me the idea, suddenly inescapable, that Keith had become addicted to Fiorinal. Though I had been watching him take it for months, it had never consciously occurred to me that he might have become addicted to his medication, that he couldn't help taking too much. It seemed logical, considering the stress he had been experiencing in the months since Brian's death, that he would have more headaches, more intense and debilitating. But when the idea that he might be addicted dawned on me, I felt as if I already knew that I was right; collecting the prescriptions over the past several months and calling the doctor, I was only confirming my suspicion.

Had Keith recently asked me to fill a prescription for him and was I struck by the local pharmacist's reluctance? Or, more likely, had I allowed myself to feel, for even a minute, my growing anger at his determined self-destruction? He's addicted to these pills, I remember thinking, right before I phoned the doctor, and I'm going to make sure that he stops taking them, now.

"My husband has been taking Fiorinal for migraines," I said, cradling the phone on my shoulder. I flipped through the stack of prescriptions. "I think he's taking too many. Is Fiorinal addictive?"

Even though I thought I knew what the doctor's answer

was going to be, I was frightened by the way he jumped on my question.

"It's highly addictive," he said. "How many is he taking a day? How many has he taken *today?*"

I knew that Keith had had a prescription filled the previous morning; it was now late afternoon. I held up the near-empty bottle of pills. Ten left. I did a quick calculation in my head.

"He's taken twenty pills since yesterday," I said.

"Good god," said the doctor. "Good god, get him up here right away. Where is he getting them?"

"I guess the pharmacy's been refilling the prescription," I said grimly.

"I'm putting my secretary on the phone; tell her you need to see me this afternoon."

Keith's lack of resistance about seeing the doctor didn't surprise me then, but it surprises me now. He must have known what the doctor's examination was going to reveal; even though he seemed to be buried under depression and guilt and the numbing effect of the pills, a part of him was already struggling toward something else. He was so tired. Physically, he simply couldn't go on the way he had. Also, I think I must have more than adequately conveyed the doctor's concern. "He thinks you're addicted," I told Keith. "He says you've taken enough Fiorinal today alone to kill yourself."

The office was empty by the time we made it up there in the crawl of rush-hour traffic. The doctor, a tall, rangy, middle-aged redhead, met us at the door and ushered us in quickly, with a kind of low-key urgency. He led us into a room and motioned for Keith to sit on the examining table, without asking him to undress or change into a gown. As he drew blood and examined him, the doctor gently, steadily plied him with questions: how long had he been taking this large number of pills; when had he begun to increase the dosage; by how much at a time; were there days when he took fewer, or none at all? Becoming quiet, he began to examine Keith's throat, he used a small instrument with a light to look into his eyes, and then, kneeling a bit and tilting Keith's head back, he looked into his nose.

"Christ," he said softly. He stood up straight and stepped back from the examining table.

"How long have you been using cocaine?" he asked. His large hands, which up till that moment had been moving over Keith in a constant diagnostic caress, were now still at his sides. "How much do you use?"

I had felt cocky, up to that point, almost triumphant about having recognized Keith's problem at last, and bringing it out into the open. I was in control, taking care of business. If the problem was Fiorinal—not just a state of mind—then the straightforward solution was that Keith stop taking it. But cocaine.

I had thought I had it all figured out, thought I saw the problem fully and completely in the clear light of my discovery. But all I had seen was a glimmer, and a dim one, of what lay ahead.

My thoughts were dark at that moment, but my blackest thought was this: that Keith had slipped so far away from me, I would never know him at all.

Sitting there in the doctor's office, holding my winter coat folded neatly over my lap, I felt ashamed. In the same way that I had been unable to seduce my father out of his grief, unable to charm Keith out of his silences and into life, I had again failed.

8

I took meticulous notes during the weeks I was trying to find a psychiatrist to treat Keith. He needed to be hospitalized in order to safely reduce his dependency on the Fiorinal. As I outlined information about one specialist and then the next, carefully noting referrals and comments various doctors made about potential treatment, I felt as if I were constructing a fence, slat by slat, around the chaos that emanated from him. I needed to confine it in this abstract way, but I also sensed that Keith needed to be physically confined—not treated as an outpatient— before he or anyone else would be able to get a handle on what was wrong with him and how to fix it. Some doctors couldn't see us and offered the names of others they thought might be helpful. Together Keith and I saw several of these, in interview sessions, but I left unsatisfied and frustrated, feeling that it had been too easy for Keith, with his thoughtful, quiet answers, to put one over on the doctors. They didn't seem to take his trouble seriously enough; after all, he had shown up for help. But Brian had shown up for help, too. Besides, they didn't know, as I did, that at some of the interviews, Keith was high.

The doctor I settled on was young—about our age, straightforward, and ambitious about Keith's treatment in a way the others had not been. It seemed to be a job to him, and he was going to get it done. It was that, his ambition and his confidence about meeting the challenge, which made me feel hopeful. He thought Keith's problem with drugs was secondary to his depression; he wanted to get him safely off the barbiturates first, in the hospital, and then begin working with him as an outpatient. He would get Keith a bed immediately.

My relief was tempered by the fact that Keith was not going directly from the doctor's office into the hospital. In the time it would take to go home, pack a bag, and make a few work-related phone calls, he could change his mind about getting help, maybe disappear. I said nothing about that as Keith prepared to go into the hospital, slipping a few things into a small canvas bag, but I watched him, guarding a growing, vicious determination that I would not let him get away. . . .

He did not get away and didn't even try to; I think mainly he was tired. When we had signed enough papers that I thought it would be a problem for Keith to change his mind about staying, I left him in the hospital admitting office and told him I'd be back that evening during visiting hours. Sitting low in the back of the taxi on the way home, and looking out the window at the gray, raw November afternoon, I felt desolate and afraid. I didn't really know much about Keith's new doctor; for no reason I could get a handle on, I didn't trust him entirely when he described Keith's treatment. (It didn't occur to me then that my trust in the medical profession might be wavering on account of Keith's experience with the Fiorinal doctor. He hadn't informed Keith that the pills he had prescribed for his migraines were addictive.) The confidence that had made me feel encouraged when we first met him seemed threatening now that he was in charge. "I needed to remove the left side of his brain," I imagined him saying. "Look, did you want him to improve or not?" Of course, in another context—the context of my feelings toward Keith—the idea of removing half of his brain—or, preferably, all of it—gave me great satisfaction. I was only vaguely aware of my growing anger at him, about not being the man I'd wanted him to be, and more immediately, about leaving me alone to raise our son, while he set about in the most determined way to destroy his life.

As relieved as I'd felt finally getting Keith into the hospital,

I now felt guilty also, as if he were handicapped and I'd institutionalized him instead of taking care of him myself. I reminded myself that he was out of control, that I'd tried to take care of him and failed, but that failure stung me, too: for the first time in my adult life, I felt completely empty of resources, vulnerable, helpless. I prayed that seeing Keith in the hospital that night would make me feel better.

The hand-lettered sign on the wired-glass door to the floor where Keith was staying read: PLEASE CLOSE DOOR QUICKLY! ELOPEMENT RISKS! Several pajamaed patients lingered in the hallway near the door. I followed the doctor closely as he let himself in with his key. It was all I could do to keep from grabbing the back of his jacket. "Wait here a minute," he told me, once we'd gotten inside. I looked around and tried, unsuccessfully, in my jeans and parka, to appear inconspicuous.

Somewhere down the hall a deep, authoritative voice was chanting, "Hell, no! Hell, no! Hell, no!" at his own private demonstration. A couple of female patients shuffled by in slow motion hugging the wall, their bandaged wrists like gauzy cuffs poking from the sleeves of their robes. A huge, bearded, bearlike man in a yarmulke lumbered along beside them, the fringe of his prayer shawl swaying below his hospital gown. He argued fiercely with himself. I thought, this was where I'd hoped I'd feel safe knowing Keith was? This ghastly place of drooling, glassy-eyed, staggering lunatics?

As I waited for the doctor, one of the patients approached me. He was exactly my height, with a patchy buzz cut. A thin white crust outlined his lips. I steeled myself, hoping that he was going to ask me a question I could answer easily (are you a doctor? a nurse? a patient?), and then move on. He put his face up terribly close to mine.

"What color are your eyes?" he asked. His tone was passionate. I thought his craziness might be contagious, carried in the strong, sickening gusts of his breath, which had a dense, plastic smell like factory fumes.

"Green," I said. I tried not to breathe.

His sharp, serious stare snaked through my green eyes, down my throat, and pricked the bubble of fear that had been rising steadily from the pit of my stomach. I began to tremble and took a step away.

"It's all right," he said miserably, "I'm sorry."

"No, *I'm* sorry," I said, feeling weak and disorganized. He brightened up. "So . . . wanna fuck?" he said, rolling his hips suggestively. He put out his hand to touch me, and I almost screamed. Where was the doctor? Where was Keith?

"Move it along, please," said the doctor, from behind me. It took only this little fillip of authority to get him going. "See you around," the patient said, winking as he scuffed away.

"Oh, God," I said, turning to the doctor. He looked ridiculously handsome and composed in his tweed sport coat. "I'm scared," I said. I wondered, do they give shock therapy here?

I pictured Keith strapped to a table, his head shaved in many small round spots for electrodes, biting on a rubber bar, while wild currents shot through his brain. A few weeks earlier I might have relished this scene. Tonight, it terrified me: too real.

"Let's go this way," said the doctor. I followed him past the nurses' station. The women looked exquisitely clean and ordinary; I wanted to nuzzle their snowy-white sleeves. We walked by the TV room, where the cigarette smoke was so thick, the cracked orange upholstery seemed to be smoldering and the patients in their blue-and-white diamond-printed robes wandered like phantoms.

"Just in here," said the doctor, at the next door.

Keith had a private room—thank god, I thought—and he slept. I stood in the doorway for a moment, not knowing whether to wake him. "Go ahead," said the doctor, nodding toward the bed.

I walked over. "Keith," I said softly. I touched his head. His hair was dirty and stiff; he must not have showered for days.

He started to puke the moment he woke up. The doctor quickly handed him a small, plastic-lined wastebasket. When he was through, Keith wiped his mouth with the sheet and lay back, exhausted. He opened his eyes for a second, saw me, and wiped his mouth again, hard, with the back of his hand.

"The vomiting is from the phenobarbital," said the doctor. "If he stopped taking Fiorinal and we didn't replace it with decreasing doses of another barbiturate, he might have convulsions or some other serious withdrawal symptoms."

I couldn't tell if Keith was listening. He lay without moving, breathing shallowly, his eyes closed, trying not to vomit, I guessed. I sat down gingerly at the foot of the bed and put my hand on his leg. I gave his calf a little squeeze to try to get him to look at me.

"I feel like shit," he said, without opening his eyes.

"So when is he going to start feeling better?" I asked the doctor, turning to face him and pushing myself off the bed.

The doctor shrugged. "In a few days," he said. "He should be out of here in two weeks."

My heart sank. Now that I could see that Keith wasn't being tortured—at least not in the way I had imagined—I didn't want him to leave the hospital. I didn't want to be waking up alone again at three A.M., wondering if he were dead somewhere, or whether he'd lost his wallet and keys, leaving Reid and me vulnerable to whoever found them.

For months, Keith had been losing things. Mostly it was

just a pain in the neck: canceled credit cards, stop payments on checks. But one morning before dawn I was awakened by a phone call.

"Keith there?" said a male voice, quiet and even.

"No." My mouth was dry. My heart pounded so, the pale light in the bedroom seemed to pulsate. "Who is this, please?"

"I've got his wallet," said the man. "You his wife? You want it?"

"No," I told him. "Keep it. Give me your number and I'll have him call you." If he's not dead, I thought.

"I'm unloadin' a flower truck around the corner," he said. "At Paradise. I'll leave it at the store."

I felt safer then; I knew Paradise would open around six; I could manage for a couple of hours till I could get over there to pick up the wallet. But what if the guy thought about the possibilities? What if he also had Keith's keys? What if he thought there was a woman alone at Keith's address, and maybe some money—I glanced around the bedroom—not to mention stereo equipment? I went into Reid's room and locked the door. I would wait there till daylight.

There were many nights like that before Keith went into the hospital, of waiting, of an acid, gnawing dread that ate away at my sleep and my hope that Keith would pull himself out of his misery. But all that fall he was absent both night and day more and more frequently, until he disappeared for days at a time getting high and coming home sick and wasted, unable to talk, unable to eat, hating himself. "Talk to me," I said. "Cut out this shit and talk to me!" But Keith was tired, and staggering under the weight of depression and grief and drugs. He couldn't respond. Quickly, I accepted his silence: I was afraid, if he did speak to me, of what I would find out. I clung to my ignorance like hope. Keith was getting royally high, and I was the Queen of Denial.

I made him milk shakes with ice cream and eggs and always asked him what I could get him, did he want anything else? I couldn't acknowledge that I knew very well what he wanted. He wanted to join his brother. He wanted to die. And if that was all he wanted, he would succeed.

9

Once the drug withdrawal became tolerable, Keith seemed completely content on the psychiatric floor. He spoke of the other patients, most of whom seemed dazed and disoriented to me, as if they were normal, as if slitting your wrists in the bathtub or swallowing a bottle of pills were a perfectly ordinary thing to do. I both admired his acceptance of these frightening people, and worried that it meant he was as crazy as they were.

He seemed happy to go out with a counselor and a group of patients to choose a buckle for a belt he was making for Reid in Arts and Crafts, and told me with enthusiasm that he had found one in an antique shop near the hospital. "I think Reid will like it," he told me. He leaned forward in the hospital chair; his eyes were actually shining. "It's got a little horse with wings etched into it—a Pegasus, you know. It's really unusual. Do you think he'll like it, Val?"

His description of the buckle and the care he put into tooling the leather on the narrow little belt were more heartbreaking to me than anything before, including whatever sorrow he had been able to express about Brian's death. Though I understood the project's therapeutic value, the dignity he brought to it seemed too large, too grown-up, and serious. In the year before Brian died, Keith had been winning design awards regularly. What was the matter with him now? Couldn't he see how pathetic it was to be tooling a belt in Arts and Crafts?

But when Keith showed it to me one visiting day, I dutifully admired the belt and his choice of buckle, and told him, yes, Reid would love it. I had just bought him a pair of trousers with loops and having a belt his dad made would make him happy.

I brought the belt home for Reid that afternoon. He and his baby-sitter were playing school, sitting on a couple of overturned paint cans in front of a small blackboard propped up against the couch. There was a big "R" on the board, and a couple of aim-less-looking scratch marks next to it. "Look what I brought you," I said to Reid as I shrugged off my coat. I took the belt out of my bag. "It's a belt Daddy made for you in the loony bin."

Reid accepted the belt and examined it closely. "Da?" he said to himself. Then he pulled it around his waist, struggled unsuccessfully to push the end of the belt through the buckle and, after I'd helped him, sat back down seriously on his paint can to continue his studies. The belt drooped slightly over the back of his corduroys, puffy with diaper. The next day and for days after, he did wear his new belt with his elastic-waist Osh-Kosh jeans rolled up at the cuffs. The first couple of times I helped him on with it, I was struck by the thought that I'd never expected to see our little boy in a belt his father had made for him in Arts and Crafts. But threading it out of the loops on Reid's trousers one evening as I was getting him undressed, I looked at how well-made it was, how symmetrical the design, and I felt happy to recognize Keith's old determination to do things thoroughly and beautifully. That determination was part of who Keith was to me; it differentiated him from other people in my eyes, made him special. The belt wasn't really useful in holding up Reid's pants, I thought, picturing the way it gripped his bulg-ing toddler belly or slid stiffly down below it like a leather Hu-laHoop; but it did hold up my small belief that underneath Keith's sickness—or beyond it—there was still a part of him I knew.

I watched Keith for signs that he was getting better during his stay at the hospital. His psychiatrist was optimistic; once

Keith was off the Fiorinal, he thought, continuing psychotherapy would help him out of the depression deepened by his brother's death. The psychiatrist believed that after the depression was dealt with, addiction would no longer be a problem for Keith. I tried to believe this, to be hopeful, but something nagged at me: it wasn't going to work this way . . . the cocaine and its connection to his brother was a bigger problem than the doctor thought. As the date for Keith's release approached, I couldn't see much of a change in him. He was off the pills, but he remained as remote as ever.

Bringing him home, I continued to try to convince myself: you knew it wouldn't happen overnight, he needs to grieve, give it time.

One morning not long after Keith returned, I ran to his desk at home to pick up the ringing phone and saw, as I pulled out a chair, a small, round mirror, dusty with coke. I stared at it as a straw rolled off the chair and dropped onto the floor.

First, furious, I phoned Keith, to tell him that I knew. He was laconic. "Sorry, hon," he said.

"Asshole!" I slammed down the receiver and then phoned the doctor.

"Keith's getting high," I said. Goddamit, I thought, *do* something about it.

The doctor was silent for a moment. "I wonder why," he said.

"You're the doctor."

"Can you get him to come to see me with you?" the doctor asked.

Later that day, Keith and I sat in his office while the doctor proposed his plan. Keith would enter a monthlong inpatient drug-dependency program; the doctor would see him nearly every day; and good news! Our insurance covered the hospital costs and there was an opening right away. The doctor had the paperwork already prepared. All Keith had to do was go home to get some things he'd need for his stay.

This time, Keith was more reluctant. A month in the hospital, with no possibility of parole. He had things to do, he thought. To me, the month stretched out like a shimmering oasis, dotted with weekend visits of limited duration. It meant rest, no more worrying about whether Keith was dead or alive, and his doctor or a social worker seeing him every day. A lot of this turned out to be a mirage, but it was a tantalizing one.

I was desperate for Keith to enter the program.

"I really don't want to do this," he said, looking at his feet.

I was ready to leap out of my seat, grab him by the ears, and twist his head around until he agreed to go. My pounding heart seemed to be pumping all of the saliva out of my mouth. But I remained quiet as death, shifting glances back and forth between Keith and the doctor.

"Look, it has to be your decision," the doctor said reasonably. "I happen to think it's the best thing for you. But you have to want to go."

What was I going to do if he refused? I knew, even though I didn't want to admit the possibility: I would make him leave the house, I would change the locks, and I would say good-bye to my marriage. The thought of that scenario made me feel nauseated and for a moment I thought I really was going to vomit. I inhaled deeply.

"I'll go," Keith said. "I guess I'll go."

The doctor moved quickly, as if he were organizing a sting operation. "I'll meet you back here in an hour," he said. "Here's a list of the things you'll need.

"Good decision," he said firmly, to no one in particular, as he let us out of the office.

A letter from Keith, just before he went into rehab:

Dear Val,

I want to get totally straight; I want to be close to you and to Reid. I want a good business that I can be proud of. I know I can only have these things if I am straight and deal with the issues before me and stop running away from my fears. . . . I know I can do it and I know you're right to keep your distance now.

I think you've been heroic; I love you for caring about me; I admire your strength and I'm jealous of your courage and your commitment. . . . You are the most wonderful parent I've ever seen—and I'm jealous of that, too, of how much of you Reid shares. . . .

So I will go into rehab to clean up and deal with my depression and put my beliefs into practice. I feel positive about this now, more than anything else, because I have seen that the people around me care about me—especially you. I'm sorry it's been so hard for you. I guess I've still needed to punish myself, but I'm very tired of that, and I don't want it anymore, at least not as much as love.

I love you.

As I read Keith's letter, years later, a rush of sympathy for him—for both of us—began to rise in me. How could I not remember that he had acknowledged what my presence had meant to him? And then I got to the postscript:

P.S. After I wrote this I started getting into work and I did some more coke to keep going. Does that make this all bullshit? I feel more pressure than I can deal with to complete the studio. It still seems endless and worse, there is really no money left to tie up the loose ends. . . .

More than anything, I hated Keith telling me while he was high what I most needed to hear. It was a terrible kind of betrayal: he knew exactly what I wanted and then delivered it in a way that was unacceptable.

We were on our way back to the hospital, downstairs, just outside the doorway to our building, when Keith stopped walking and put down his bag.

"I don't think I want to do this," he said.

I stood there next to him on the freezing street, needing to scream. *Shit!* Keith, I said to myself, grinding my teeth and looking away, this is up to you. I want you to get help, but if you are determined to kill yourself, then fuck, that's what you'll do. Suddenly, unexpectedly, as if I had been dipped in it, I felt a wash of calm: what Keith did was beyond my control. "Okay," I said, "let's go back upstairs." I opened the front door. "Come on."

He picked up his bag, hesitated, took a step toward the door.

And then he turned around.

Remember when we were downstairs that day, on the way to rehab, and I said I didn't think I wanted to go?

Yes, Keith.

Well, I wouldn't have gone if you had tried to force me. I needed to feel as if I had a choice about what I was doing. I knew it wouldn't ever work if I were doing it for you.

In the hospital admissions office for a second time, I felt as if Keith were an undergraduate beginning school. The admissions counselor explained the rules of the rehab, running through them quickly, very matter-of-fact and understated as if it would never occur to someone like Keith to even consider breaking any of them. By the end of his spiel, when he reached into a lower drawer in his desk, I thought he was going to give Keith a freshman beanie; but he pulled out a thin white coffee mug with something inscribed in green on one side. "This is for you," he said to Keith. "I'm giving it to you now to take home with you when you've completed your stay here." Then, maybe because he didn't understand why neither one of us reached for it, he added, "It's free." Just what we needed, a mug. He put it in Keith's hand; we silently read the inscription together:

> *God grant me the serenity*
> *To accept the things I cannot change,*
> *The courage to change the things I can,*
> *And the wisdom to know the difference.*

If Keith and I had been alone, I would have stuck my finger down my throat and gagged. But because the counselor was looking at us expectantly, as if he had given us a gift he hoped we would like, I did my best not to appear ungrateful. My best wasn't very good in this case; I raised my eyebrows, nodded, made a kind of "Huh, isn't-that-interesting?" sound, and looked quickly away. Keith, always and increasingly less concerned than I about what kind of impression he was making, sat holding the cup, staring at it and shaking his head. Oh, God, he was thinking, here it comes. This is where they start inculcating me with T-shirt slogans.

My worry was more general. How, I thought dismally, was this ever going to work?

It was beyond my understanding how profoundly Keith's treatment was going to affect me. I continued to think of his illness as a contained thing; once he got rid of it—his addiction, his depression—he would be better, and then our lives would be normal again. Well, normal; normal wasn't something I thought I'd cared for, until we had the baby. Then, I'd been overcome with a lasting, postpartum craving for structure. I wanted a nine-to-five kind of life, I wanted to know I would get up to the same thing every day and do the same thing and see my husband walk through the door at the same time at the end of the day and say good-night to him, too, every night. I wondered at the fact that when I married him, I thought my choice in Keith was safe, more than anything. He seemed not to need to take unreasonable risks, he ran a healthy, thriving business, and he had seemed in so many ways predictable. He wasn't at all ordinary, but still he was safe. How did it come to be that two years into our marriage, I never knew what would happen next?

The letter read:

Dear Valerie Monroe,

"Family Week has been scheduled for December 23, 1985.

Your patient is involved in this treatment program because of a chronic illness—harmful dependency on a chemical substance. Chemical dependency is also a family illness. This illness is a destructive force in both the patient and other family members. The family is adversely affected, and before treatment is considered successful, family problems must be recognized and addressed.

. . . There is group therapy each day for family members, designed to help family members recognize and acknowledge their feelings, defenses, roles, attitudes, and thus gain insight into their interaction with the chemically dependent person and with each other.

. . . Involvement in the treatment process is critical and may necessitate changes in your daily routine. We realize that this is difficult and involves sacrifice and inconvenience. However, this is one of the most important time investments you will ever make. . . .

Family therapy. I hated it. It was excruciating. I held a nasty grudge against Keith for getting me into it; if it weren't for him, I thought, I wouldn't be required to share my feelings with a group of people I never saw before, and hoped I never saw again, or have to listen to their nauseating problems. The listening was easier than the telling, when I could think of what was going on as a kind of living theater. But some of what was divulged was so undiluted, so bitterly painful, that it seemed to sear my insides as it went down. I was afraid I wouldn't be able to metabolize it, that it would sit like a burning weight on my stomach and make me sick. I often did feel sick during the sessions and afterward, and couldn't wait to get outside the hospital where I would take big gulps of cold air.

But worst of all, I was expected to give feedback. We were instructed as to how to respond in ways that were constructive. For example, we were not to give advice, but to "confront" instead. It was not acceptable to say, "You shouldn't let your mother speak to you that way." We were supposed to say, "You seem like a baby letting your mother speak to you that way." This was to get a person to be able to see himself from another point of view. We were given other examples: "You seem hostile because of your sarcasm." "You seem self-centered because you only talk about yourself." And we were told, quite rightly, I thought, after hearing the examples, that it took courage to risk confronting someone. I thought of the ways I might confront Keith: "You seem angry and depressed, because you are trying to kill yourself."

It was difficult for me to understand how such confrontations were going to advance Keith's recovery or strengthen our relationship.

In fact, the therapy increased the intensity of tension between everyone. A small group of patients and their families—parents, spouses, adult siblings—would file in, behaving civilly at least, take their seats on opposite sides of the room, and within the hour they would be inflicting incredible pain on one another, lobbing insults, hateful memories, devastating accusations. The emotional land mines were so abundant, so explosive and so surprising, that I was sure there would be casualties. During their family sessions, the smoldering father of a recovering heroin addict would get progressively redder in the face till his veins stood out like a pulsing purple map across his forehead; it seemed it would be only moments before he'd explode and the whole messy geography of his emotions would splatter across the room. I had never seen such display; it fascinated and terrified me.

I understood the value of venting, of being able to have one's feelings in a safe place, but it seemed then that all of this airing was only fanning the fires of despair. I yearned for a tidy Miss Manners to replace the frayed counselor who led the group: instead of asking me, as he absently picked on his flannel shirt cuff, "How do you feel about what Keith just told you about the money he has spent on drugs these past few months?" she would fold together her smooth, white hands and say primly to Keith,

"Speaking publicly about how much money you spend is . . . indelicate."

Yet, I was also grateful to find out what exactly had been going on. At the time I didn't know, or suspect, that I was only learning a bit of what Keith had been doing to himself—more details would come later.

"At family week was the first time I saw Keith since Brian died," their sister, Maggie, recalled. "I was so scared. I was scared Keith was going to kill himself, too.

"Do you remember when I was crying and I told Keith how worried about him I was? Do you remember what he said to me? He said, 'You're just afraid that what happened to Brian and what's happening to me is going to happen to you next. You don't really care about me or Brian. You're just afraid *you're next.*' "

I hadn't remembered those words, but when I did, I instantly recalled Keith's face as he spoke them, and his nightmarish transformation. His eyes, normally deeply expressive, turned steely, reflective, impenetrable; his mouth hard and despising. He looked utterly like a different man. Seeing this transformation— and the despair it caused in Maggie—was terrifying.

That, in fact, was one of the most harrowing things for me about Keith's addiction, that the Keith I thought I had loved disappeared. Imagine someone close to you—your husband, or lover, your child—recognizable from the back; the familiar slope of the shoulder, the way he rests his weight on one foot, all of the welcome invitations to expect the face you know, to see your feelings for him reflected in his eyes. You call his name, he turns: the features are familiar, those features you love, but the eyes are blank, the look is cold, as if the person inside has vanished.

10

For about a month, beginning in early December when he entered rehab, Keith slept in a dormitory arrangement with three other patients. To call me at home, he had to use a public phone in the hall that was nearly always busy; because I could only see him on weekends, and then only for a limited duration—I usually brought Reid with me—our contact was minimal. Visiting hours were chaotic. The combination of the smoke, the noise, and a frenetic energy made it impossible for us to talk and I felt as if we were continuing to grow apart. Still, I would tell Keith to watch for us from his window after I left the hospital; I would stand in the park across the street, holding Reid, and point Keith out to him as he waved good-bye. Seeing him looking small from the distance of the park, framed in one of the narrow, dark hospital windows, stirred in me the little compassion I had for him. I think that's why I did it. But as I turned to walk away, I was always glad to be going home without him.

I tried not to make much of the Christmas Keith was in the hospital. (My family had always celebrated both Christmas and Chanukah as traditions, but neither religiously.) The holiday didn't mean anything to Reid, who was too young to appreciate it and didn't seem to be aware of Keith's absence, but it hurt me to think of how I wished the day would be. A friend who lived in the country had given us a huge wreath, which, with a large nail and some difficulty, I tacked up out of Reid's reach on one of the unfinished walls of the loft. As it hung there the week before Christmas, becoming in the overheated house ever less green and more bristling, it began to take on a kind of mesmerizing, threatening quality. I came to avoid looking at it with the same kind of purpose I would have admired a pretty, ornamented tree.

Christmas morning, after I had settled Reid at the kitchen table in his Sassy seat and splayed some Cheerios across his tray, I brought out his one present, a Bert and Ernie book that I'd wrapped in Santa paper.

"Merry Christmas, tootsie," I said. The words stuck in my throat. I wish now that I could have just sat down at the table and sobbed, but it being Christmas morning and only Reid's second Christmas, that didn't seem appropriate. Instead, I tried not to feel sorry for myself.

Reid tore off the paper viciously and flung it around him in that straight-armed way babies do; then crying, "Book! Book!" he slammed it flat on the table, crushing his breakfast and sending it flying. In a grand gesture, he swept to the floor whatever cereal remained on the table; he gnawed the book as if it were a juicy bone, drooled into it, opened it in the middle, and sat it triumphantly like an A-frame on his head.

"You like it," I said, feeling cheered.

We would see Keith for a couple of hours that afternoon, but I wasn't looking forward to the visit. I didn't want to bring him a gift, since he would have nothing for us; we didn't have much to talk about, and the hospital had been seeming especially grim. Both the holiday decorations and the patients, many of whom were heavy smokers, seemed grayish and stale. As soon as we got onto Keith's floor, I craved the fresh air outside. I didn't care whether or not he knew that I didn't want to be there.

On our way to Keith's room, several of the patients wished us a Merry Christmas, sounding gratingly, falsely cheerful. "Merry Christmas to you, too," I said, in the same tone I would have told them to take their feet off the table. I was carrying Reid on my hip; he started humping to get down, so I let him run on ahead into Keith's room. There was a small box, gift wrapped, on his bed.

"What's that?" I said.

Without answering, Keith walked over to the bed and handed the box to Reid. "Santa gave me this to give to you," he said. Reid took the box eagerly. "From Santa Claus," Keith said.

Inside was a little floppy stuffed lamb, covered with soft ivory fleece.

"Mines?" said Reid.

"Yes, honey, it's for you," said Keith. Reid snuggled it for a moment, and then put it down on the bed. He picked up the box and began to chew it wetly.

"Where did you get that?" I asked. "You didn't *make* it, did you?"

"I brought it from home," Keith said, "when I first came in here." He moved to his night table, opened the drawer, and took out two unwrapped, jewelry-sized boxes. "These are for you."

It made me ache to think that Keith had brought something to the hospital for us. But I had become accustomed to feeling angry with him and wore my anger like an old coat; it had kept me comfortable against the chill of his abandonment and I was loathe to remove it even when I knew I might be warmed instead by his generosity or an attempt to show me that he felt something for me.

He had bought me two exquisitely delicate Victorian pins. "I made them," he said in mock seriousness. I looked up at him and held his gaze. "I'm sorry they aren't wrapped," he said. I know that I wanted to cry then—I cry about it now, remembering—but I wouldn't let myself. What would happen if I told him how desperately I needed him? How desperately I wanted everything to be different? What if I told him that I never really knew how to love him and was afraid that I would never know?

It was just easier to slip into my anger. "Thank you," I said, moving away from Keith and dropping the boxes into my bag. As I sat down heavily in a chair near his bed, I felt as if I had closed myself to him completely.

I didn't know who to hate more for that, him or me.

One warm spring day years later, Keith, Reid, and I had gotten into a cleaning frenzy. In one room of the loft, designated to be another bathroom one day, we had accumulated boxes of junk—Reid's old baby clothes, some toys too babyish for a seven-year-old, boxes of records we had inherited from Keith's father—and we were going through them, saving, discarding, remembering. In a sane moment, years before, Keith had labeled the boxes carefully. I pulled out a big, dusty one; VOODOO, it said in black letters across the top.

"What's in here?" I asked Keith, half expecting to find some strange cabalistic objects: a dried-out hank of hair, a couple of teeth, ridged and brownish, an old bone. Some part of Keith's past he had forgotten to tell me about. A triplet, maybe.

Nestled inside were two puffy rubber baby dolls from my childhood. They had gotten dirty even in the sealed box. The terry robe on the bigger of the dolls had yellowed, and its pink and blue trim was unraveling. I remembered how I had cared for this doll, hid her in a little bed in the alcove of my room, always diligent about the blanket being pulled up to the doll's chin and her sleeping face turned away from the glare of the window. . . . I had begged my mother for the doll when I was twelve; she was reluctant to buy it for me, saying that I was too old to play with dolls and that I was being a baby. She didn't understand that I *was* being a baby, that doll-baby, and that in caring for her, I was playing out caring for myself.

"What's that?" Reid asked, peering over the pile of stuff to peek at my dolls. "Eww, *weird*," he said, pulling away. It *was* weird, I thought, carefully folding the flaps down to reseal the box. Not that I had saved the dolls, but that I had, at a time when most of my friends seemed happy to be discovering boys, needed this doll to take care of, to protect me against the threat of growing up, against the inevitable changes of adolescence. I thought of the day I sat with Reid as a baby in the stuffy car while Keith frantically tore through Brian's apartment, looking for something he could make sense out of, something that would help him understand what Brian had done. I knew then that that was only the first time I had used Reid in the way I had used the doll; that all through our marriage, after Brian died, I had continued to take care of him in the way I had wished to be taken care of myself and that I had used him to protect myself from everything that was difficult in my marriage.

"What the fuck?" Keith said suddenly.

"Pardon your French," said Reid.

"Excuse me," Keith said as he held up a white, business-sized envelope with ONE THOUSAND scrawled across the front. "Look at this," he said, opening the envelope and fanning out the bills. A thousand dollars. Ten hundreds. More money than Reid had ever seen at once.

"What the hell?" said Reid. "A thousand dollars? Say, what box did you get that from?" Reid scrambled over the open boxes, knocking over piles of books and scattering his old toys. "Is there any more of that in here?"

I looked over at Keith. Was there any more of that in here?

"I think this is it," Keith said. "I know I had these hidden all over the place, but I'm pretty sure I used them up."

Then I began to wonder, for the first time in this concrete way, how much money Keith had spent during the months he was addicted. Ten thousand dollars? Twenty? Thirty?

I remembered my conversation with the accountant the day

Keith went into the hospital for the second time. "You have two alternatives," he told me matter-of-factly. "You can close up the business—just let everybody go, lock the doors—and we'll declare bankruptcy. Or you can try to borrow enough money to keep it going for a month until Keith gets out of the hospital.

"But I don't know whether you want to do that, hon," he said. "It's kind of a lot of money. With the renovation and everything, he's got a pretty high overhead."

Close up the business? Declare bankruptcy? I had no idea the business's finances were in such a shambles. Because Keith had long-standing clients who gave him work regularly, as well as new clients whose work was both lucrative and dependable, and because all of his employees were still producing, I had thought the business was chugging along on its own steam. I didn't realize that without Keith to generate the work, to supervise and to be the liaison between the studio and the clients, the business would peter out, lose its power. There were serious bills to be paid for the renovation. A couple of months more without Keith's energy, and the studio would be completely inert, shiny and new and going nowhere.

After discussing it with Keith, I borrowed the money from his father and delivered the message to the small staff that he was sure that he was on the way to recovery and would be back at work in less than thirty days. The accountant had one more piece of advice. "Sweetheart," he said, "take ten thousand dollars out of the business and put it into an account in your name. Make sure that Keith can't touch it."

"Should I?" I said. "I'll feel like a thief."

"Look, honey," the accountant said, "I love Keith like my own son, but in two months I don't want to see you and the baby out on the street with no money and no place to live."

I knew I'd always have a place to live—even if it meant moving in with one of my family—but it had never occurred to me that we would lose everything. Keith was in the hospital, getting better, wasn't he? He wasn't going to go through a monthlong recovery program and months of supervised care afterward and go back to getting high . . . was he?

No, I told myself reassuringly, *no way.*

Then my instinct, my dark, unerring instinct, sidled up behind my sunny attitude and jumped it. Pocketed a wad of hope before vanishing, and whispered in my ear, *You bet.*

I put the money away.

As a follow-up to the rehabilitation program, Keith and I were encouraged to participate for two years in an aftercare group that met for a couple of hours once a week. Recovering addicts and their spouses or parents were to use it as a time to air their feelings, to express concerns or anger in a safe place. Two recovering addicts or alcoholics, trained in leading the discussion, tried to keep us all on track.

The idea of keeping an open mind about the group didn't occur to me. Everyone seemed weird at best, losers at worst; in the beginning I spent most of my energy trying to convince myself that I didn't belong there. Still, some of the couples got to me. Like Ray and Ellen, the couple who finished each other's sentences.

"I didn't want to come to the . . ." Ray said.

"Hospital," said Ellen. "He was so sure that he didn't have . . ."

"A problem," said Ray.

I sat there following their conversation with my eyes, as if I were watching a Ping-Pong match.

"I wonder if you could allow each other to finish one sentence. Just one," I said, smiling at them through transparent irritation.

"Does it bother you?" one of the counselors asked, as if it were strange that I noticed.

"I think it's weird that they talk like . . ." I paused, trying to figure out what it *was* like.

"Like our tongues are joined . . ." said Ellen.

"At the hip?" said Ray.

They regarded one another affectionately.

Ellen was a tiny, exquisitely neat, birdlike woman whose hands were raw from washing. She always carried a pad and a freshly sharpened pencil, though I never saw her take any notes. Her delicate fingers, red and scaly, curled around the pencil as she spoke, and when she darted her eyes to look attentively at other group members as they were talking, the soft plume of spiked hair above her forehead jauntily bobbed from side to side. I loved watching her; if I held out a handful of seeds, I was sure she would hop off her chair and skitter across the floor to peck them out of my palm.

Whether Ray was talking or listening, spittle collected slowly in the corners of his lips, till it began an agonizingly slow trickle down the side of his chin. Pulling sharply with his teeth on his lower lip, he would try unsuccessfully to suck it up, resorting, finally, to wiping his mouth with a soiled handkerchief he kept in his trouser pocket. I found myself salivating and swallowing in spite of myself. His rubbery, gray complexion gave him an oily look; greasy salt-and-pepper hair hung limply to his shoulders.

They were mad about one another. From the very beginning, as they talked about themselves, about their relationship, and about how Ray's addiction had brought them to our group, it was evident that, despite their problems, they loved being in one another's company. I disdained them. But I was jealous, too.

There were other couples and single recovering addicts

who passed through the group during the two years Keith and I were in it. A few, who started around the time we did, lasted with us until our time with the group was over. But there were more who came for several months only, or even several weeks, and who we knew were sucked back down into the powerful vortex of their addictions. From these people I learned more about what Keith might have been going through than from the controlled, articulate group members—like Keith—whose faltering descriptions of how they felt when they were high or explanations about why they needed to take drugs sounded both clichéd and remote.

One of the reasons I had no patience with Keith about his addiction was that I believed that he was making a choice to get high. To me, the choice was simple: take drugs or not. Period. But watching the people who were losing the battle to stay clean, listening to them offer up their reasons for getting high, which sounded hollow and pitiful and were always indefensible, I began to have an idea of the pain involved in making that choice. The pain only abated once they had picked up, and since they weren't allowed to come high to group, I saw them when their pain was most intense, when they were coming down, or knew that they were going to go back out. Though I was too angry to forgive Keith his behavior, through the other addicts in our group, I was beginning to understand what was driving him.

And it was in group that Keith and I learned how to fight. This was handy, since we fought a lot. It was simple: we never began a sentence with the word "you." When we got into an argument, everything we said had to begin with "I feel," so that we were locked into expressing only that. (A statement like, "I feel you're full of shit" was not acceptable.) Suddenly our arguments—which had always begun in long, smoldering silences, abruptly ignited into shouting hot accusations, and then cooled off into an icy distance—were turning into confessions of feelings we often weren't aware of.

"This is a miracle," I'd said to Keith the first time we ended an argument facing each other with greater understanding. I actually felt closer to him. For the first time I entertained the idea that we would be able to shape our relationship by our behavior; that our relationship didn't define us, as I had so often thought when our fighting seemed out of control, but, finally, that we would define it.

By the time we had been in our aftercare sessions for a couple of weeks, I was trying to believe the worst was over. Keith had completed the rehabilitation program; I wanted everything to slide inexorably toward swell.

But Keith seemed not to be getting better; in fact, unbelievably, he seemed to be getting worse. He was unresponsive to the counselor's gentle probing about how he was doing; he never participated in the discussion unless he was asked to, and then spoke only in monosyllables.

One evening, to everyone's astonishment, he announced that he wanted to share a dream that he'd had the night before.

Hey, I thought, progress.

Keith seemed to be satisfied that he had captured the group's attention. He spoke so quietly that it seemed as if we had nearly stopped breathing in order to be able to hear him.

"So in this dream . . ." Keith said, leaning forward in his metal chair and looking at the floor. The slowness with which he spoke was agonizing. We all waited for him to go on. He continued to stare at the floor. Chairs creaked as we shifted around, trying to discharge our discomfort. Apparently having lost his nerve, or deciding against sharing the dream, he retreated into silence.

"Keith," said the counselor, "go on, please."

"Oh, for Christ's sake," I wanted to say, "don't go on." I felt manipulated and impatient.

Keith began again in the same, quiet monotone. "So in this dream I was running from something, running and running and I couldn't get away."

"What was it you were running from?" the counselor asked.

Keith took a deep breath. "It was a death's head," he said. "A skull with black holes where the features should be." He continued to stare at the floor.

Oh, God, I thought, here we go again. Didn't he want to get better?

"Wow, man, you're in really bad shape," said one of the group, shaking his head and wrapping his arms around the back of his seat. "You better, like, you know, pull yourself together."

"Give me a break," I muttered. "Give me a fucking break."

The counselor looked over at me and raised his eyebrows expectantly. "Any more feedback, Valerie?" he asked.

"I think Keith's feeling sorry for himself," I said. "I don't think he wants to get well."

Keith shot me a murderous look.

"I think he's going to go out again," another group member said quickly.

"Speak to Keith, please," the counselor said.

The group member turned to face Keith. "I think you're going to pick up again," he said. "Have you been going to AA meetings? D'you have a sponsor? Have you been talking to anybody about the way you feel?

"Because, you know man, you sound terrible."

Keith stared miserably at his feet.

Fuck you, I wanted to say. *Can't you see that he doesn't want any help? Leave him alone,* I wanted to say, *let him have his way. Let him kill himself.*

I felt as if Keith were getting all the help available to him; I didn't know what else I could do for him, or what anyone could do. I felt the same frustration about him that I had felt about Brian: he seemed to be asking for help, and then rejecting it.

Yet, leaving him then was impossible. Whether it was true or not, I believed that Keith needed me. How could I leave him in the state he was in? Maybe more important was the sense that whatever my role was in our relationship, it wasn't resolved for me. I wasn't sure what I was doing, where I was or how I had gotten there. Even so, I always had the sense that it was important that I not give up. I was waiting for something; the trouble was, I didn't know what, exactly.

Sometimes it felt to me that we were hunkering down through a storm, Keith and I, and that one day all of the terrible, fearsome blowing would be over and the pelting rain would drizzle into a mist and then burn off, and we would see each other again, with the kind of clarity you can see in the clearing after a hard rain.

But then we lived in a kind of limbo, just getting through. I don't remember Keith ever telling me that he loved me during that time, nor I him. Our arguments, though they were fair enough, were frequent enough to be exhausting. Keith went to work in the morning, I cared for Reid; then when Reid's sitter came in the afternoon, I worked on the book I was writing. In the evenings I dined with Reid on nursery food: broiled chicken or chopped meat and potatoes. I never saw much of Keith at night. I had stopped asking him if he would be home for dinner. His design studio had become his home.

I harbored keen expectations about how Keith should behave. I told him: "Don't you get it? You're supposed to be dealing with your grief, acknowledging your mistakes, and turning your attention toward rebuilding your relationships with me and Reid. *Don't you get it?"* Then I waited.

After a few more weeks Keith did seem to be turning around, on the face of it at least; miserable as he was, he was going through the motions.

11

A couple of months out of the hospital, Keith finally seemed calmer. He had put on a little weight and appeared more solid, in my eyes, more capable of resisting the lure of drugs. Whether it was because I couldn't face the possibility that he might start using again, or whether I had the thought that he was ready to stay clean, I felt confident that something in the recovery program had taken in him. Though he was still depressed, I wanted to believe that he no longer considered drugs an alternative.

He was making the AA meetings that had been recommended to him in the hospital, and he seemed to be pulling the business along. I wanted so much to believe that Keith's time in rehab had "cured" him. The alternative scared me deeply. I continued to think of our problem in terms of "Keith's illness," which, in fact, would limit my ability to find ways to deal with it.

On Valentine's Day, he handed me an envelope. Inside was a card with a sepia photo of a large brush of tumbleweed, blowing across a sandy field. Heavy clouds hung over the landscape. "Dear Val," the card read, "You're the tumbleweed in my desert. I'd be empty without you."

"Really, Keith?" I asked. "Is that the way you feel?"

He drew me to him and held me in his arms, so tightly that he trembled.

When he said he was going downtown to an AA meeting one evening as he helped me clean up after dinner, I had no inkling of his plans; there was nothing in his tone of voice or his look or in the way he waved bye to Reid as he let himself out the door that he was on his way to meet his connection. As he was leaving, I thought, this isn't so bad, maybe we can move ahead from here; maybe we *will* be able to make something out of this.

I went to bed alone at midnight, not having heard from him. I had the chills, and a familiar jittery feeling in the pit of my stomach. I woke up at four, the dim light in the bedroom still on, Keith's side of the bed empty. A cold fury began to spread through me, till my feet and my fingers felt like ice and even scuttling way down under the comforter I couldn't get warm; I was cold all over and numb and finally I kicked off the covers and started pacing around the bed. "This is crazy," I said aloud. "Am I crazy? I must be crazy." From my bureau I snatched a black-and-white framed photograph of Keith, taken before we were married, when he looked clear-eyed, gentle, and promising. I held the picture up at arm's length. "Do me a favor, you shit," I said. "Get it over with." After one abbreviated burst of tears, I let the photograph fall to the floor. I hoped it would break. It didn't.

Then, grabbing my robe, I went out to the kitchen and started some coffee.

By the time Reid woke up, squawking happily for a bottle, I felt thin-skinned and hollow; I had sat in the living room watching the night drain out of the blue-black sky till it was a lifeless gray, the same exhausting phrase spinning over and over in my mind: *What do I do now, what do I do now, what do I do now?* At least with Reid up, I had to direct my attention to him.

"Hi, baby," I said, going into his room. He held up his arms to be lifted out of his crib and clutched me around the neck like a little monkey. The weight of him in my arms felt good, proof that I was still functioning.

Mechanically, I unsnapped his pajama bottoms, got him

into a dry diaper, carried him into the kitchen, gave him a bottle of milk, which he sucked greedily, and sat down with him in front of the TV. Mister Rogers, mesmerizingly deliberate, spoke to us good neighbors as he changed into his sneakers. I began to feel seduced by his fuzzy goodwill, the sound of the baby sucking next to me; my shoulders dropped and I drifted.

A surge of fear, hot and electric, nearly lifted me off the couch when the phone rang. The baby popped the bottle out of his mouth and watched me as I walked quickly into the other room.

"Hi. It's me," Keith said, his voice low and tired.

"Where are you? Are you all right?"

"I'm all right," he said. "I didn't want you to worry."

"I *was* worried," I said urgently, "I *am* worried. What's happening? Where are you? What are you doing?"

Keith was silent.

"Are you high?"

Still silence.

"Keith, where are you? Are you high?" Suddenly, without warning, I started to cry, a flash flood of tears that filled me up fast and spilled over onto the phone. "I love you," I sobbed. Then I felt guilty. I wasn't sure anymore that I did.

"Just don't worry about me, hon," Keith said, and hung up.

I winced at the click of the disconnection, and continued to cry as I put down the phone and walked back into the living room. Reid turned away from the television to look at me as I sat down in a chair near the window. I thought at first that he thought I was laughing, the way he waddled over to me, half smiling, with his bottle tucked under his arm. But then I saw that he had cocked his head to one side the way you do instinctively when you're trying to get a handle on what someone else is thinking, as if the perspective from a slightly different angle will help you understand.

"Oh, baby," I said. "I'm sorry." I was afraid that my being upset would upset him, too. "I'm feeling sad," I said.

He leaned against my lap and offered me up his bottle.

"Sure," I said. I took a couple of halfhearted sucks while he patted my thigh.

"Whew," I said, wiping my eyes. "Whew. It's all right. I'm all right. Let's get you something to eat."

As I scrambled some eggs for Reid's breakfast, I tried to make plans for the day. I would call Keith's doctor, I would take Reid to the park . . . and I would do something I had dreaded and put off for months. I would leave Reid with his sitter and go to an Al-Anon meeting. Just to see what it was like.

And besides, I finally conceded: I needed to get *myself* some help.

I chose a group that met around the corner from where we lived, thinking that it wouldn't be worthwhile to travel more than a few blocks, since I probably wasn't going to stay long, anyway. The room, in a church basement, was wood-paneled, stuffy, depressing. There were framed, hand-lettered slogans perched along the wainscoting: FIRST THINGS FIRST; THINK, THINK, THINK; ONE DAY AT A TIME. Ten rows of folding chairs faced a large, heavy oak desk up front. A woman about my own age, sitting behind it, was speaking quietly to the group; a few looks strayed my way when I entered the room but when I quietly slipped into a seat against the wall in the back, I felt safely unnoticed. The woman continued talking, quickly, intensely.

I looked around the room and listened. It was hard to get the gist of what the woman was talking about . . . she spoke so quietly and urgently, and after a few minutes she began to pepper her dialogue with bursts of repentant tears ("It was so awful, how could I have done it, what could I have been thinking of?").

What *was* she talking about? A priest, I got that much, and something about wanting to get closer to God, and then as I was scanning the room—judging the women by their hairdos and handbags—I heard her very clearly say, "So I fucked the priest because I wanted to get closer to God, and now he doesn't want to see me anymore and I feel so . . . *abandoned."* Head down on the desk, she began to weep in earnest. No one said anything. I realized I was sweating, probably from an effort to keep myself from bolting out the door. This meeting was, in every way I had imagined and more, as bad as I thought it was going to be: the depressing room, the simpleminded slogans, the pathetic Al-Anonics fucking priests to get closer to God. . . . At least I'd have a good story for my friends, I thought, relieved at the idea of being able to make fun of it.

After she had pulled a wad of Kleenex out of her sleeve, wiped her eyes, and blown her nose purposefully several times, the woman up front said, "I guess I'm done, thank you." There was weak applause, and then the only man in the room stood up at his seat. He was graying and unkempt—there were shopping bags, stuffed and torn, around his chair and he wore a couple of watch caps stacked on his head. The room was warm; was he going for the aesthetic?

"I have some announcements to make," he said, and when he was through, he asked, "is there anyone new to Al-Anon in the room?"

A couple of women raised their hands. I did not.

"Hi, welcome," he said, pointing at one woman and then the next, as each introduced herself by first name and said something brief about why she was there or how she felt. When the last woman had spoken, he turned his gaze on me. I locked my eyes with him, hoping to stare him down.

He seemed absolutely impassive. "I haven't seen your face before," he said solemnly. "Would you like to say something?"

Oh, fuck. My stomach churned. I pushed my chair back up against the wall.

"I didn't want to come here," I said. "This room is depressing." I became aware that everyone had turned around in their seats to face me. "I mean, I thought you'd all be assholes."

The man in the watch caps nodded thoughtfully.

"I can't speak for the rest of the room," he said. "But I know you're right about me."

A few of the women laughed. With what—scorn? Affection? The woman sitting next to me gently touched my arm. "Come back," she said. "Just give it another try."

I looked at her closely, scanning her outfit to determine her level of sanity. She looked like somebody's mother—my mother, actually—and for just a moment I felt comforted. But not enough to stay. The members of the group now madly waved their hands to be called on, frantic to relieve themselves of their stories, like schoolchildren needing permission to pee.

"I'll try to give everyone a chance to speak," I heard the woman behind the desk say weakly as I closed the door after me.

Leaving the dingy church basement and stepping into a shower of clear, bright afternoon light, I felt almost clean again, rinsed of the musty neediness I had felt inside. I remembered my seventh-grade dance classes, where the skinny girls like me stood against the aluminum folding chairs, smoothing our white cotton gloves and waiting to be chosen to dance . . . and waiting and waiting, till the class was finally, thankfully over. In my mind, the women in that basement were all those little girls who had never been asked to dance, or who had been asked by the wrong boys; I had spent my life running away from them and I didn't want to believe I was one of their company again. But I knew very well who they were.

I realized, walking home, that I had never told my story,

Keith's story to anyone. "Come back," I heard again in that motherly voice.

Four days had gone by with no word from Keith. When-ever the phone rang, though I hoped it would be him, I expected the police. I was supposed to be working on my book project, but I couldn't work. I didn't want to talk to anyone; I felt on the verge of something unpleasant all the time, that irritated feeling you have before you jump into a cold pool when your body anticipates the shock but isn't yet required to respond to it.

Keith's absence in the house taunted me. In the morning our bed, a comfortable jumble of quilt and pillows when Keith was there, took on a cryptlike quality; I slept so still that when I got up, it hardly looked as if the bed had been used. It made me sad to realize that because Keith and I had been spending so little time together that I had, finally, become attached to his impression in our bed. At least I knew he had been there. Now his side, flat and cold, stared back at me as soon as I opened my eyes, a smooth, unrumpled blankness, reminding me that he was gone.

I clung to my routines with Reid, packing him up in his stroller and taking him to the market, home for lunch, to the park if the weather allowed, sometimes feeling, as I stood behind him, pushing him gently in a steel swing at the playground, or sitting with him on the living room rug, rolling a ball between us, as if there were another me in my head, watching me play with Reid and crying, because there was a part of me that was crying, always, during that time. The face I showed to my son and the rest of the world was a coping face. I made an effort to act as if everything were fine because I didn't want anyone to know what a failure my marriage was.

I cried aloud in bursts, after Reid was in bed, or when he was napping and I had a couple of moments alone. I might be fixing myself a sandwich and thinking of something cute Reid had said or done when I'd slip into imagining I was telling it to Keith—not the Keith who was out there being destructive, but the Keith I wished for, a loving, interested Keith—and suddenly, as if I'd been jolted out of a dream, I'd wake up to the reality. The contrast was so harsh that it made me weep. I cried because I was alone with a baby, because I was frustrated that nothing semed to work for Keith, because I thought I had made a stupid choice in marrying him, because I was tired. I felt no sadness for him. Sometimes I secretly hoped that he would kill himself, so that I would be free of him, so that I could go back to being the remarkably happy, together person I thought I'd always been, and go on.

But what if he's dead? But what if he's already dead? That thought rose up ghoulishly, wrapping itself around every other thought I had. I remembered that a couple of years before, Keith had been jumped late one night by a gang of kids who demanded his money. "Fuck you," Keith had said. The kids swiftly beat him up and left him bleeding on the sidewalk. A ragged flap of skin hung from his chin as he wandered the streets trying unsuccessfully to hail a cab. He found his way, finally, to a hospital emergency room, where his face was stitched, he was given painkillers, and sent home.

He'd seemed such an easy victim, perilously undefended. His hostility invited violence. That is how I thought of him during those four days; there was something about him that said, *I don't care if you hurt me.*

He'd told me he'd had a regular connection who delivered him drugs. There oddly seemed a kind of safety in that to me now, as I pictured him scoring instead from strangers wanting to rip him off or hurt him just for the hell of it, any of his instincts for being careful and sensible depleted. The more I thought about it, the more possible it seemed that this time, if Keith made it, it was going to be close.

I didn't tell my family about what was happening because I didn't feel like suffering through their sympathy. I didn't call Keith's family because I didn't want them to worry. To the other mothers of the babies in Reid's play group, whose husbands changed diapers and, if they didn't help with dinner, at least showed up for it, I was silent. Around them, I felt as if there were something the matter with me because my husband was sick. (Actually, there was, of course, but I hadn't figured that out yet.) If I were smarter, or more well-adjusted, or stronger—or maybe just luckier, I thought—I'd be married to a man who wasn't losing his mind. Or if I were, at least I would know how to help him find it. As we chased around after our kids in the park, or in one or another of our living rooms, I listened sadly, enviously, as they talked about supper with their husbands after the babies were in bed, or debated about whether or not to have another child.

I felt more comfortable with single mothers then, those who were also raising their babies on their own.

And I kept on going to Al-Anon meetings.

The faces in the rooms were different, except for Watch caps, always there with his bags, but the medium was the same: church basements, folding chairs, slogans on the walls. At one meeting, the speaker, whose story I had missed, looked like a young ad executive—in a pastel cloud of a suit, tasteful jewelry, two hundred dollar haircut, smart skin. Even as I was aware of the shallowness of my judgment, the way I tallied up and admired the sum of her assets, I took comfort in the way she looked. She was calling on people as I took a seat. I listened as everyone in the room took a turn speaking.

"Anyone who hasn't shared yet?" asked the speaker.

I raised my hand.

"Yes? In the blue shirt?"

"My name is Valerie," I said.

"Hi, Valerie," said the group. I hated that part: saying my name, and hearing it repeated with conscientious kindness. I felt reduced, clarified, as if all there was of me was this quivering jerk whose life was out of control. There was a soft, shuffling sound as everyone in the room turned around to look at me. I sat with my hands clasped in my lap.

"Last summer my husband's twin brother killed himself," I began. I glanced at Watch caps, who was writing something in a tiny, black notebook and didn't appear to be listening. "Now I think my husband might kill himself, too," I said. "He's taking drugs. He's been in and out of the hospital. It's very hard for me to watch him; I don't know what to do."

I took a deep breath. "I guess that's it," I said. I glanced at the faces around me, sympathetic, expectant. I added. "We have a baby." And then, looking down at my hands because the sympathetic faces were making me want to cry, I said, *"I'm afraid."*

I sat still in my chair. The attention in the room remained focused on me during the silence before anyone else spoke. My heart had been thumping fast from nervousness as I talked; now, as it slowed, I sensed my feelings catching up. Something inside me had moved. I felt as if the group were holding my story— which allowed me to loosen my own hold on it, let them have it a little, and gave me the opportunity to see it as they might see it. I felt something new, unfamiliar and strange: an inkling of compassion. For me, for Keith, for the people whose pain had brought them here.

"Yes?" The speaker had called on Watch caps. He spoke forcefully to a spot in the room above our heads.

"One of my most favorite, simpleminded slogans is, 'Don't just do something; sit there,' " he said. "It's never the best time for me to do something when I'm unsure about what to do." He read from another small book he held: "This is today's entry in the *One Day at a Time* book," he said. " 'I pray to be released from my compulsion to control my situation. I have so often proved I am unable to control it. Let me think, know and feel my powerlessness; then I will at least learn to let go and let God.' "

I fought it, but I began to cry. I knew that my constant efforts at constructing a plan were like a dam against my feelings: if I quit trying to figure out what to do, I would be flooded with fear.

The woman sitting next to me put her arm around my shoulder. "It's hard," she said. "I know it is."

Late one afternoon, one of Keith's employees phoned. Keith had called her. She knew where he was.

"He's in a Midtown hotel," she said. "He wants me to come to see him. He wants me to bring him some food. He sounds sick, Val," she said worriedly. "He sounds like he's dying."

"Don't you remember?" Keith said to me, when we talked years later about the last time he went out. "Don't you remember what you told me the morning I called?"

"I don't remember telling you anything," I said, truthfully. "I only remember crying."

Then Keith told me that he had decided that night that he was going to get high—but only for an hour. (How do you do that, I wondered? He might as well have told me that he believed he was going to be a woman for an hour.) "Then, of course, I was out all night," Keith said, "but I thought I was through with it. When I phoned you in the morning, I was at the studio. I was going to tell you that I was finished with drugs for good.

"But you told me not to come home. You told me I couldn't come home until I had been straight for twenty-four hours. Because I didn't have to come home for you, I realized I could go out for more.

"If I hadn't done that, I'm sure I would have come home and gone out again another time, because—I didn't know it then—I wasn't finished at all."

I had told Keith not to come back. We had agreed when he left the hospital for the second time that if he got high, he couldn't come home till he'd been straight for at least twenty-four hours. That saved me from having to deal with him when he was high, and it also made it clear to him that he could not be doing drugs and see his family.

How could I have forbidden him to come home that morning? Part of me was glad to do it: I was angry that he had broken his promise to stay straight. Yes, I was afraid that all he needed to hear was that I didn't want him back—for any reason—and that might push him over the edge. But I also hoped that he would get close enough to dying that he would know that he didn't really want to. I simply couldn't imagine that he wanted to die. When his employee phoned to tell me that she had heard from him, I begged her not to help him, not to take him food. I had a very clear intuition that he had to reach a crisis before he would be able to begin to work toward a resolution, and that he would survive that point if he chose to. I told myself he would make a different choice than his brother.

12

When he returned, Keith was thin again, pale, almost translucent in a deathly way. I expected to be angry with him, but when I saw him I was not. His frailty protected him from any outbursts from me.

He came back early one afternoon when I was out with Reid. Though there was no evidence that there was anyone in the house when I came in off the elevator chatting with Reid and pushing the stroller ahead of me, I knew instinctively that Keith was home.

"Just a minute, baby," I said to Reid as I parked him near the elevator door. I left him there, strapped into the stroller in his jacket and his hat, as I walked quickly down the hallway. "Mommy'll be right back in one second," I said.

Seeing no one in the kitchen or the living room, I moved cautiously into the bedroom. Keith stood in front of an open drawer of his bureau, holding a clean undershirt. He was scrawny and tired-looking. His hair was wet from the shower.

"Are you straight?" I said from the doorway.

"Yes," he said, keeping his eyes on mine. "I'm finished with it. For good."

Reid began yelling for me from the front of the house. Reflexively, I made a move in his direction, then stopped. "Keith," I said. He looked at me. I felt that stinging in my nose that signaled I was about to cry. I took a breath. At that moment my fury at him was imprisoned by relief. "I'm glad you're back." Then, because I didn't want him to see me crying, I turned and ran out to get Reid. I was so afraid to let myself go with Keith, to let him see the part of me that I was just beginning to acknowledge. I was afraid he wouldn't like it, wouldn't like me that way, with nothing to offer him but my feelings.

"Daddy's home," I said to Reid as I lifted him out of the stroller and unzipped his jacket. "Daddy's home," I said again as I plucked off Reid's hat and used the fuzzy blue pom-pom to wipe my eyes. I sat down cross-legged on the floor, crying into the hat, as Reid trotted happily down the hall toward his father, calling "Dad!" and waving his arms in front of him.

There was another reason, besides his frailty, and my relief, for my equanimity around Keith. In the week that he had been away, I had begun to change, too. In spite of my discomfort with and my contempt for Al-Anon meetings and the people in them, I had forced myself to go every day. It was the only useful support I had. I'm not sure how conscious I was of this then, but with each meeting I was opening the door a crack more to the unwelcome idea that I, and not only Keith, needed to change. This adjustment, at first though it was only minute, of the focus of my attention from Keith's problems to my own had a remarkable effect. Keith, without the unremitting spotlight of my expectations trained mercilessly on him, was becoming just another character fumbling along in the dark, like me, in fact, trying to make the connections that would help him understand how his life had gone so painfully awry. Freed from trying to figure out what was making him unhappy, I began to take a look at what was making me unhappy. I felt as if, for all of my life, I had been wearing glasses with the wrong prescription; after slipping on a different pair, every time I turned to examine something new, it came vividly into focus.

My mother suffered from eczema during her entire pregnancy with me. Nothing seemed to clear it up; ointments, medicinal soaks, milk baths, even a nine-month-long psychoanalysis, were useless against it. Just after I was delivered, the rash cleared up.

"You see," my grandmother told her, "all you needed was a little girl to make you feel better."

That innocent pronouncement, maybe more than any other, shaped my childhood. Making other people feel better was something I learned how to do well; it was my full-time job. It validated me, made me believe that I deserved a place in the world. One of the nonnegotiable terms of my employment was that other people's wishes and ideas were more important and valuable than my own. Who was my boss? Anyone but me. I was always a tributary, feeding other people's needs.

In reading the literature of Al-Anon, and listening to the people who participated in that program, I began to consider how assuming the role of caretaker had become destructive for me, how I used it to make myself feel strong, rather than develop other, more positive and creative ways. I noticed my compulsion to try to fix a relationship—which usually meant that I became conciliatory—whenever it moved in a direction that made me feel uncomfortable, whenever anger or any agitating emotion began to seep into an otherwise placid connection. After a while, I was able to see this pattern, understand it, and, because it no longer felt comfortable, stop it. But it seemed a long time before I knew what to do instead. Being in that state of suspension was extremely difficult; I had my relationships spinning swiftly like plates on sticks all around me, but I had no idea how I was to keep them going as they inevitably began to waver.

I watched and waited, feeling anxious. I was silent when previously I would have jumped in to move a conversation away from a confrontation. I was silent when there was a hole in a conversation, when I would have tried to fill the space. I discovered that my silences were like a mirror, allowing me to recognize myself, my presence amidst the myriad feelings that emanated from any relationship. Witnessing my presence disentangled me; it wasn't that I began to stand outside my relationships, but that I was able to stand in them, and yet be able to see through the fog of my habitual responses to my true feelings. And then I saw that not only were my own feelings clarified but that I was recognizing the feelings behind other people's responses, as well. It was as if the real world had opened up for me, and everything that I had heretofore perceived as real was either only subtext, or defense. I was beginning to enjoy moments when I felt thoroughly different, when I thought I knew how it felt to be an adult.

According to Al-Anon precepts, what allowed me to do this was called "detachment"; for people living with addicts, active or recovering, it was the key to survival. If there is any reason for my happiness, besides Reid, in the aftermath of Brian's death and Keith's addiction, it is that. Detachment cultivated a space between me and Keith uncluttered by expectation. And what eventually grew there instead, to my wonderment, was compassion.

In the end, too, the Al-Anon meetings served another purpose for Keith and me. Because Al-Anon is a kind of companion program to AA (its purpose is specifically to support the families and friends of alcoholics), it uses the same vocabulary. When Keith and I were both attending meetings regularly, we became comfortable with the same language—the very language, in fact, that we had gagged over not six months before. We were now both playing the same game, but in different fields, with different teams, and because we were neither competing with each other nor demanding of one another that we play the game according to the other's rules, we were free to enjoy it. Sometimes we did enjoy it.

In the months that I continued to go to meetings, the complexion of the group began to change. It was not only that I was meeting more people, more varied in their backgrounds, and many coming from situations more similar to my own, but I was also seeing them differently. Watch caps, as strange and offish as he was, nearly always contributed, in his flat, nasal, disconnected way, a piece of wisdom that floated with me, like some fragment of an inspiring song, throughout the day. I was grateful to have met him.

And there was safety in those rooms. I came eventually to look forward to the lunchtime meetings I made in my neighborhood, where office workers, neat and organized-looking with their trench coats and briefcases, seemed to carry in with them some of the comfortable, unvarying structure of their jobs. The contrast between the straightforward, adult lines of their appearance and their vulnerable, messy, and often childlike expressions of fear, or grief, or gratitude was stark and compelling.

In Al-Anon, I began to accept these people who didn't meet my expectations of perfection; who had failed at things that might have been important, but who had the courage to try to face their limitations, or to move beyond them; people who had never trusted their feelings, who had been taught to hide them and who were now learning to share and respect them. Gradually, as I accepted these others, I was learning to accept myself.

"My husband's a drug addict," I would say, when asked who my "qualifier" was, the person who was my reason for going to meetings. For a long time, I said it blamefully: if it weren't for Keith, I said, I wouldn't be here. But a year later, as I had begun to appreciate what I had learned and my relationship with Keith had begun to change, I started to think of it differently. If it weren't for Keith, I thought, I might never have come this far.

After Keith returned from his slip back into drugs, I knew I wasn't going to allow him in the house if he had been high, according to our agreement, but aside from that, as much as I could, I tried to let my expectations about him lapse. For now, I was going to do what I had to do to make myself happier; what Keith did was up to him.

We continued with our aftercare group. I had attended our meetings alone while Keith was out on his slip. I had felt triumphant about Keith not being there. *See,* I had wanted to say, *I'm a good girl, going to aftercare and Al-Anon meetings. Keith's a fuckup, isn't he?*

The counselors were grave at the first meeting Keith made, but welcoming. I was detached.

But something in Keith, too, had begun to change. He said, for the first time, "I'll go through hell before I take drugs again." He began to share in aftercare meetings, not in the halting voice I had become used to, but more confidently. He began to allow himself to experience his pain.

That allowance marked the beginning of his recovery.

"Did you and Brian ever say you loved each other?" I asked recently, thinking about how often I have made that declaration to my own brother and sister.

"Not as adults," Keith said. "Not that I can remember. But I *felt* it whenever I saw him. And I knew he did, too."

Their coolness with one another wasn't just masculine reserve. He'd always felt that he wasn't supposed to show his love for his brother, Keith went on. The boys' father, demanding, authoritarian, and, it seemed to Keith, often oppressively controlling, discouraged spontaneity. Their mother, first with two babies, and then another one four years later, predictably must have found raising three kids without any help difficult and exhausting. Brian claimed that one of his early memories was of their mother scrubbing him and Keith with a scrub brush when they were two or three—for shitting in their pants—and locking them both in a closet. The twins were rarely rambunctious when they were together, Keith said, because as children they had to be manageable, most of all. They weren't allowed to be high-spirited; it was most acceptable for them to be quiet and serious. In that dampened state was where they felt safe expressing their connection.

Keith remembered that one of his aunts had once said to him, "You boys were so good, it was scary." And then went on to tell him about them visiting her when they were about eight and how she asked them, when she left the room for a few minutes, just to stay where they were. She was gone for more than a few minutes, she told Keith, longer than she expected, and when she returned, fifteen or twenty minutes later, Keith and Brian hadn't moved, were exactly as she had left them.

I sat with Keith in silence for a few moments, thinking of that and feeling sad.

"I thought I could connect with Brian if I could understand his pain," Keith said. And then, thoughtfully, "I think that was why, after Brian died, I needed to feel what Brian felt, to know what he went through.

"It was the only way I knew to keep my connection to him alive.

"I had spent nearly every day of my life with him until we went away to college," Keith continued, and then grew quiet.

Keith found it difficult to describe their relationship. It was a given, it was always there, like the air.

"I thought my grief would destroy me," Keith said. "I wouldn't let myself feel it because it seemed so overwhelming. I thought it would be . . . endless."

"What is your relationship," he said, finally, *"to the part of you that just is?"*

I thought of the grace of Keith's struggle, the terrible emptiness after Brian's death, and his later resolve to learn something from it, to live in a different way.

"After I left rehab," Keith said, "I was sure that I could stop when I wanted to, but the last time I went out, I found out that I couldn't."

"But after what happened to Brian, how could you ever think you could control the drugs?"

Keith snickered. "I had plenty of reasons to think I could. But the main thing was, I wasn't Brian."

"But so what made you understand that you weren't in control?"

"How sick I got," Keith said. Then: "I wanted to reach the very bottom of my addiction, to look death in the face and say, 'Fuck You!' That would somehow make things right with Brian. It would give me back the part of myself that I had surrendered out of fear."

I watched my husband's face.

"I grieved for Brian partly because I couldn't save him. But much more than that, I grieved over the fact that I didn't know myself, that I had lost the connection with those parts of myself that would have allowed me to be with Brian when he needed me.

"My greatest loss," Keith said, "wasn't that I couldn't love Brian. Because I did. It was that I couldn't express my love to him and allow it to shape our relationship.

"In my addiction, I was trying to catch up with him, to be with him in his pain, to share it with him."

For the first time, I was beginning to understand something of what Keith had experienced.

"Beyond that," Keith continued, "I now had the perfect excuse to be bad, to rebel at the self-control that had limited my experience for so long. Not only would I say 'Fuck You' to death, but I could say it to life, too.

"Brian's death made me aware that, like him, I had lost my connection to myself."

In a less acute, but equally profound way, it had done the same for me.

Not allowed back home, Keith had scored some coke, re-filled an old prescription for Fiorinal, taken a room in a hotel, and set to work at the business of getting high. The more coke he blew, the more excruciatingly his head hurt, and so he swallowed more pills. Finally, he realized that his body was shutting down, that his heart would freeze. "I thought, Yes, I can actually kill myself," Keith says now. "That slowed me down. I thought about what I felt in the morgue with Brian's body: What a waste. What a terrible waste.

"And then I just saw very clearly my addiction as empti-ness. There was nothing in it for me. It was endless. I believed that even after I died the feeling of emptiness would go on.

"And I knew that's not what I wanted. I deserved some-thing better.

"It was over," Keith says. "I knew I wasn't going to take drugs ever again."

Keith got sick then, with fever and sweat and chills, and he lost his voice, and he did sound as if he were going to die.

But he knew he would not.

Years after that, I tried to imagine what it would feel like to have to try to decide whether I wanted to live or die. All I could think of was our son.

"Keith," I said. "Reid was just a baby then. Weren't you thinking about what it would be like for him to have to grow up without a father? Didn't you want to see him grow up?"

Keith shook his head. "Active addicts don't think about anybody but themselves," he said. "I never thought about Reid."

I remembered the despair of a young woman in our after-care group who shamefully, tearfully, spoke of locking herself in the bathroom so that she could shoot up while her three- and five-year-old kids cried for her outside the door. How could she? I remember thinking, but her self-loathing was so strong, I only wished that she would forgive herself. It was easy to understand the frighteningly fine line between acknowledging her pain and living with it and succumbing to the need to deaden it with drugs.

Thinking of that, I looked over at my husband. Just at that moment, I saw him not as my Keith, but as a person unencumbered by his connection to me, someone who had suffered and struggled. He had had a choice: to let his pain drive him, either completely or discreetly, or to face it and walk through it. Sensing the courage it took to do the latter, my heart swelled with admiration for him.

13

Keith resumed the routine of the studio so quickly after his slip that it seemed as if he hadn't really been gone at all. I had had a meeting with his small staff after he'd phoned me the week he'd disappeared, when two of his six employees threatened to quit. "I don't know what to say to you," I told them. "I can't blame you if you leave." I felt my throat tighten. "But please. Give him one more chance." My hands shook as I zipped my jacket when I got up to go. I desperately didn't want to break down in front of this little group; I was afraid they would feel sure that there was no point in staying, that the situation with Keith was completely hopeless if his wife had lost hope, too.

The staff did stay on, and if they welcomed Keith back warily, they were soon too busy with work to dwell on whether or not he was back for good.

With one of Keith's clients in Santa Fe, he had to fly out there occasionally to finalize jobs. When he told me, nearly a year out of rehab, that he was going to have to make a trip, I was relieved. The tension between us was exhausting; even though we were both trying to make the marriage work, it was still usually much easier when we were out of each other's way.

Every small annoyance was magnified by my resentment: he left on the bathroom light because he knew I wanted it off; he loaded the dishwasher the wrong way; he cut his hair because he knew I liked it long; he coughed in his sleep. When I pointed out to him all of the things he did to harass me, he had the audacity to feel picked on.

After his trip Keith had gone, at a friend's suggestion, to see a guy in Chinatown who read his tarot cards. He said he had done it on a whim, just for fun, but I suspected that he was also searching for something. He had taped the session. I asked if I could listen to the tape, thinking that Keith would tell me, sure, okay, I don't care.

"No," he said flatly; no explanation.

"No? Why not?"

"I'm just not comfortable with you hearing it."

"What specifically are you uncomfortable with my hearing?" I asked.

"It's personal."

"Personal?" I said. "What is it you don't want me to know?" I flipped through the possibilities in my head alphabetically, like cards on a Rolodex. Drugs? Leaving me? Lost money? Sick?

"Have you had another slip?" I asked. I had followed him into the bedroom, where he was getting ready to go to work. Still in my robe, I sat on the bed. He faced me.

"All right," Keith said. "I thought I found the woman I wanted to spend the rest of my life with. She was the AA contact in Santa Fe. That's what's on the tape I didn't want you to hear."

Here is the point in the story where it might make most sense for me to be writing, *So I packed up my things, grabbed our son, and left.* "I hope you'll be very happy together," I might have said, or on the other hand, "Rot in hell, shithead."

Here was my opportunity, laid out before me like a new suit. I might have slipped it on, fastened my belt and buttoned the jacket smartly, said good-bye, and walked out of the marriage into a different life. Who would have blamed me? *He thought he fell in love with another woman,* I'd say. *After all I'd been through with him, he fell in love with someone else.*

But all I could think was, No fair! No goddam fucking fair!

"It was an infatuation," Keith said. "I don't feel the same way about it now." I started to cry. "Val, I was on a business trip. I met someone. We didn't even do anything."

"Leave me alone," I said. I crawled under the covers and pulled them up over my head.

Keith stood helplessly at the foot of the bed. "Val," he said.

This isn't the way this relationship is going to end, I thought. Him being stupid and cruel and me feeling victimized. We are both better than this, I remember thinking. Why is this happening?

Keith took Reid to preschool while I stayed in bed and cried. I dwelt on that phrase I so often heard in Al-Anon: keep the focus on yourself. Dear God, I prayed, please help me to learn something from this. I repeated that entreaty like a mantra. A couple of hours later, feeling sick and weak, I got up. I had to pick up Reid at school.

Writing about this now, I worry about not being able to explain why I stayed. There was an element of fear, an old fear of not being good enough for a relationship with a man who cared for me, who felt committed to me. But what was most painful to me at the time, as I remember it, was that I *had* stayed with Keith, and in fact still wanted to stay with him, despite how unhappy he had made me. What would make me want to do that? Some of my friends might have said that I stayed because I loved him, but I couldn't say truthfully that I did. I'd thought I did, but I had lost track of what it was that I thought I'd loved. And now I couldn't let go of the idea that he was in love with a woman in Santa Fe, even though he had told me with finality that he did not want to pursue the relationship.

All afternoon I felt sick with revulsion for not having the brains, or the guts, or whatever it was I needed, to leave him. When Reid's sitter came in after lunch, I asked her to take him out to the park; "I need to work," I said, feeling ridiculous because my swollen eyes clearly indicated that work wasn't likely to be on my agenda that day. I tried to concentrate on one of my freelance assignments, but when I had to call sources for interviews, I either couldn't make sense out of what they were saying, or their quotes seemed vacuous and silly. I couldn't ask an intelligent question. I couldn't write. I despised myself. I finally gave up and went into my room. When my lungs hurt from too much crying, I took deep, hiccuppy breaths and told myself, I need to learn something now. Help me learn something.

Keith came home from the studio after I'd gone to bed. That night I slept hard. In a dream cloud, I sat between my parents, the three of us visible from the waist up and surrounded by beautiful pink and gray vapor. I leaned toward my father and kissed him. Becoming aroused, I kissed him more deeply and more deeply still, till I began to feel as if I might go into a swoon. Suddenly, I felt my mother's presence, and I drew away, frightened and then angry.

I woke up the next morning perspiring and disturbed, remembering the vivid picture of me and my parents, but mostly the intensely uncomfortable dream feelings. I put my pillow over my head, as if I could muffle them, but my unconscious went on delivering. I began thinking about the relationships I had had with men.

Pulling the pillow off my face, I stared at the ceiling. Could this be right? I went over the four lasting relationships I had had since high school; the men were very different, but they had one thing in common: when I met them, they were all involved with another woman.

"Holy shit," I said out loud. I was on to something big. I felt both queasy and awed, as if I were staring straight down into the craggy chasm of my neurosis. I covered my head again and slowly pulled the pillow back as if to see if my feelings would still be there in the light. They were. But as I lay there thinking about the dream and the connection I had made, I felt something else, too. Hope.

Keith's infatuation no longer seemed very important to me. Though I couldn't then have articulated why, I felt as if I had been handed a gift, as if something promising and important awaited me.

That morning I phoned a therapist. "I need to see you," I said. "I have some work to do."

The operative word, I think, was "conflict." I was stuck in a kind of grinding competition with my mother for the attentions of my father—or any reasonable facsimile of the two, witness my string of still-attached boyfriends.

As long as there was another woman in the picture, I could allow myself not to be in a relationship wholeheartedly. I was only the half-girlfriend, the half-wife, the not-quite-entitled. If I never said what I wanted, I never risked not getting it.

The process of freeing myself from this pattern was deeper and more complicated than I could have imagined. Before I began working on it, I could only understand it from an intellectual point of view: I have this problem with the way I behave, I will think about it differently, so I will behave differently.

Instead, I found myself wandering through a vast, hoary purgatory of feelings, joined by a therapist who, having previously journeyed through similar territory (either with other patients or in a textbook, I wasn't sure), enthused over the (often unlovely) sights, reminded me of their remarkable (to him) historical significance, and encouraged me along just as if we were together discovering some fascinating foreign city.

We had begun to draw a pretty fine map of my emotional

terrain. For the first time in my life, I knew how I had gotten from there to here. And also for the first time, I had a good idea of where I wanted to go. I allowed myself to experience the feelings for both of my parents—the yearning and disappointment, the anger and the love, the sexual feelings—that I had shut away in the dark. I had been afraid of what would happen if I brought them out and looked at them, but as I did, and realized each time that when I examined a feeling I didn't explode, or die, or get set upon by wild dogs, I began to acquire a fearlessness. Which isn't to say I wasn't afraid; but that I would consciously put the fear aside. Then I knew my fear was not me, but something separate. I could move beyond it.

I had always believed that love came from outside of me, that I needed to do something to earn it, to be loved. Consequently, I was perpetually judging myself: was I good enough? Kind enough? Smart enough? Love, for me, seemed always about to be revoked.

The feelings I uncovered and then talked about told me a story about the child I had been. I found it impossible to listen to that story and not feel for her: she, like my son, was so full of innocence and love! And so, coming through each therapeutic session, there I sat, rewarded and comforted by my own compassion. It felt as if I were now both remembering and raising myself. I remembered my innocence and my hopefulness, most of all, and recognized in my adult self the ways I still often carried those attributes as unselfconsciously as a child. I was raising myself up by being the parent I had wanted, understanding, caring, forgiving. As the child felt accepted by the adult, and the adult by the child, I understood that the love I felt was not being donated to me, but moving through me. The more I experienced it, the more there was, as though the act of feeling it generated more. All I had to do to have it was to remember myself.

I had discovered my one, true, real boss.

I stood behind Keith at the bathroom sink as he shaved. "This is it," I told him, as I faced him in the mirror. "I want to try to make it work, but differently now. I'm stepping into this marriage with both feet. I'm asking you to do the same. I want you to make up your mind. Are you in or out? If you're in, I have to have your wholehearted commitment to work with me. If you're out, we'll deal with it." As I looked at him, his face full of lather, his mouth open in surprise, I already knew that he had made up his mind. He put down his razor.

"I'm in," he said.

"Both feet?"

"Both feet."

Keith had gone to Myrtle Beach for a long weekend, to a spiritual center where he could meditate and revive his connection with the teachings of Meher Baba, the Indian spiritual master he had been involved with off and on since college. It was the first time he'd gone back there since Brian died. I hoped Keith's time away would help to strengthen him. When he phoned, late on Saturday night, I knew that something was up. There was a catch in his voice, some excitement. He began to tell me about visiting an old woman at the spiritual center who had spent time with Baba. His feelings were extraordinary, he said. He was so moved by her, felt so happy in her presence.

There was a loaded silence.

"You're going to India," I said.

"How did you know?"

"It just flew up and hit me in the forehead. When do you want to go?"

"Next week," Keith said.

I was quiet.

"This is really, really important to me," Keith said. "I need to do it. Val?"

Why, then, didn't I say, "Enough of your needs, to hell with your needs!" Why didn't I say, "You come home right this minute and start acting like a husband and father!"

I know if I had said that, Keith would have come home. But the truth was, at that moment, I didn't want him there.

I thought ahead to the three weeks he would be away, which happened, I realized, as I glanced at the wall calendar near the phone, to include Reid's birthday in February, and one image filled my mind. It was that of me, heavily muscled, wringing Keith's neck.

"Keith, damn it, I want to kill you," I said. "It's not fair, you going away and leaving us." Then I thought about how much easier it was for me when Keith wasn't around. Life with Keith was tart; I craved him in small doses, but after too much of him I could feel myself beginning to pucker around the edges. I sighed. "But I also want you to go." Once I'd said it, I was sure it was the right thing. I'd get more time with a sitter for Reid while Keith was gone, so that I didn't feel stuck. I thought again of the weeks ahead, imagining having the house to myself, with no expectations of Keith coming in or going out, of never having to deal with him. I liked doing things my way, with no interference. And I loved being alone; I was, in fact, quite happy for a temporary break.

After we said good-night and hung up, I leaned against the kitchen counter and rubbed my eyes. I had a selfish reason for wanting Keith to follow his heart. It would either lead him toward me, or away from me, but either way, it would lead him where he wanted to be, and I thought that that promised a conclusion.

Maybe Keith would go to India, find whatever it was that

he needed, and come back a happier man. Or, I thought, as I made my way to the bedroom, stepping on a small, sharp piece of Tinkertoy along the way, maybe he would go to India, find whatever it was that he needed, and stay there.

All I yearned for was one or the other, I thought as I drifted off to sleep that night: a happier marriage, or none at all.

When Keith first told me that he was a follower of Meher Baba, soon after we met, I was indulgent. An Indian spiritual master? That was quaint. My father had been interested in Eastern religions when he was a young man, and as a child I had thumbed through a few of the books he kept from that time: *The Third Eye,* and *Autobiography of a Yogi.* I didn't understand then what the books were about, but there was magic in them for me. After my father died, when my mother and brother and sister and I were going through his books and deciding which of them each of us would have, I took those two. Though I'd hoped Keith's interest wasn't too much more than a casual pursuit—I didn't want him turning into a glassy-eyed bliss junkie—I loved it that he was searching.

Keith showed me a black and white picture of a middle-aged man with long, wavy hair reaching his shoulders. His eyes were compassionate and inviting. "This is him," Keith said.

I recognized the banana nose and goofy grin. I'd seen his face on posters. "That's Meher Baba?" I said. "Isn't he the 'Don't worry, be happy' guy?"

"There's more to him than that," said Keith.

"Did you ever meet him?"

"No. He dropped his body in 1969."

"He dropped it? Where?"

"That means he left his physical form," Keith said.

Oh, God, I remember thinking. Is this another can of

worms? Keith told me then about his beliefs: that Meher Baba was the avatar, the Supreme Being, God, and that he was the latest of many incarnations of that Being—Zoroaster, Rama, Krishna, Buddha, Jesus, and Muhammad being some of the others. He told me about Baba's writings, explaining the ways in which he believed the world was ordered.

"Okay," Keith said, getting down to business, "now, there are seven spiritual planes."

"Can you get a direct flight?" I was compelled to ask. Keith rolled his eyes and resumed. He talked about souls being in various stages of development, about reincarnation, about what I interpreted to be a kind of currency of the soul called sanskaras, and showed me a card that listed some of the ways one might love God. Except for the how to love God stuff, which was on the "love they neighbor" theme and commonsensical, the teachings seemed like a lot of hocus-pocus. Karma? I thought. Not that old thing!

Keith tried occasionally to get me interested in something he was reading about Baba; I would make an effort to listen, because he was so enthusiastic, but soon either my eyes would glaze over, or I'd become more interested in Keith's enthusiasm than the material he was reading from. What was it that excited him about that particular piece of information? Well, Keith would say, it's important because . . . and then he'd go into a long explanation that left me fidgeting and wishing I'd never asked.

Eventually, he brought out his Baba books less and less often, till he hardly talked about Baba at all.

Keith's interest in Meher Baba resurfaced after he began to recover from Brian's death. Most of my friends and my family found his involvement weird—or at least, unusual. But now, for me, it had taken on a different cast. Whereas before Brian died I thought of Keith's interest as fanciful, I now thought of it as a bridge for him, a way to maintain his connection to his brother and feel at peace with himself. When anyone asked me about it, I'd shrug. "Whatever gets him through," I'd say. I felt more understanding about Keith needing to find meaning or an order in the world that suited him, and also happy that the way he had chosen was working for him. The more I saw that it helped him, the more positive I felt about his choice.

It'd been a miserable winter and I was complaining to Keith one morning as I brushed my teeth about the fact that it was already April, and the mercury was still barely making it to forty degrees. Keith stepped out of the shower.

"The weather's messed up, isn't it," he said thoughtfully as he toweled off. "That's because there are so many unnatural sanskaras in the world that the angels can no longer control the natural forces."

I spat loudly into the sink and turned around to look at him. I couldn't tell if he was baiting me. "Is that really what you believe?" I asked.

"Well, it's one theory."

As I rinsed, I thought about the fact that I was married to a man who actually entertained the idea that seraphim controlled the weather. What did that say about me? Was I just open-minded, or foolishly permissive? I couldn't decide. I finally came up with a satisfying bottom line: at least Keith didn't believe that *he* controlled the weather. I walked over to the shower and kissed him on his bare shoulder.

"That's a nice theory, hon," I said.

I was determined that Keith would spend more time with us when he returned from his trip. Not so much for my sake—though my craving for him always increased the less I saw of him—but for Reid's. I thought, enough already Keith, now that you're back, be back! It's time you started to take some responsibility for your son. I hadn't pushed the issue—first, because for a time Keith was incapable of caring for a child, second, because he always seemed inundated with work, which was, after all, what paid the bills, and third, because I liked making all of the decisions about Reid. Now I had decided that I wanted to try to start sharing some of that responsibility; I thought Reid would benefit as well as I.

The evening Keith came in, Reid and I were playing a quiet game of Chutes and Ladders on the living room floor; Keith breezed through the door, dropped his bags, and moved so swifty over to us that I hadn't time to get a good look at him. After we hugged, I stepped back to take him in. In his canvas cap with the visor and his navy short-sleeved polo shirt, he had that lightly toasted look of a happy camper who has just spent three idyllic weeks at sleepaway. He was boyish, and buzzing with the spiritual high that had overcome him in India.

As he unpacked his shoulder bag, setting out some Indian coins for Reid, some amber and lapis beads for me, he talked about the long trip over, and the wild taxi ride from Bombay to Ahmednagar, eight hours away, through streets teeming with people and chickens and oxen. "It's another world over there," he told us, shaking his head. Then he told us about the first time he had gone to India, when he was still in college in the late sixties; how he had sold his childhood stamp collection and flowers on street corners in order to raise the money to go. How, on arriving at the ashram, he had walked up the small, dusty hill to the samadhi—the tomb—where Baba was buried, and sat down inside. And how as he sat there, layers began to fall away from him, layers of fear, of sadness, of anger, of confusion, till all that remained of him was his naked heart, open and pure and full of love. He felt safe, he said, open and full and safe. On this trip, it had happened again.

I watched Reid lay out his coins in a neat circle as I listened to Keith. I wasn't sure what to say to him. Everything I thought of resonated with a kind of greeting card tinniness: "That's great, honey." "It sounds very moving." "That must have meant a lot to you." Finally, I looked at him, glowing golden in the fading winter light. I scratched my nose. "Gee," I said.

It wasn't that I didn't understand what he described. But it was so far, so different from what I had been experiencing during the weeks that Keith was gone, that I couldn't focus on it; it was as if I had spent the past three weeks studying all of the obvious, practical minutia of home, solid and clear, and now Keith was showing me something thousands of miles away, flickering and ineffable.

But he seemed happier, calmer than before he had left. I hoped it would last. I wanted his happiness for him and for me, of course, but I also wanted it for Reid. I was never sure how much Reid knew about what was going on with his father or with the two of us together, but he often said things that indicated how much he had absorbed. When I told him that Keith wanted to take him to the park the weekend after he returned from India, Reid, struck by the rarity, asked me why.

"Because Daddy loves you and he wants to spend some time with you," I said.

Reid fixed me with a look. "I think it's because he loves *you*," he said.

"Well, you know, he loves both of us, honey," I said, and then fell into my worried state about how Reid was making out. I wanted so much to do right by him. All during Keith's illness and afterward when it was a struggle between us I worried about my focusing too much on Reid, about Keith's ignoring him, and more generally, about genetic predispositions to addiction and suicide. How could I protect him?

I watched Reid for signs that he was too good, trying to make life easier for me. He was reasonably considerate, but clearly focused on his own needs. I watched for signs that he was angry, not able to express it, or sad or anxious. He was angry, sometimes, and then I wondered was it normal and did I need to be especially concerned? But what I saw was that Reid was a lot better than I was most of the time at expressing what he felt. I tried to encourage him without being intrusive. I loved him so much; I wanted him to understand how joyful his *being* made me feel. I wanted him to love himself.

Though the happiness that I felt when I was with Reid was unrivaled—or maybe it was because of that—I needed time independent from him, especially when Keith's illness necessitated my taking care of him and the business. But also I felt it important that Reid be free of me; my feelings for him were so intense that I was concerned they would overwhelm him, or me. How were my feelings influenced by the imbalance of the relationships in the triangle of our small family? I couldn't know the answer to that; the best I could do was to keep asking myself the question and explore the feelings that it aroused. I knew that I wanted Reid to be able to count on me; with his father so often out of the picture, it was crucial that he have one parent consistently there for him. But as passionate a parent as I?

From the time Reid was about eight months old, I had arranged to have a sitter come weekdays in the afternoons; she was a young woman, playful and kind, and by the time there was big trouble, she had become a fixture for Reid, someone who he knew he would see every day and who was consistent in her affection toward him. Though I gave her some of the facts of our problems ("Keith's twin brother died." "Keith's ill and has to go into the hospital."), I didn't share the details. I thought she might become frightened, as I was, and I didn't want her to leave, or her fear to influence her behavior with Reid.

But I think of the years I spent with Reid, as he developed from infant to toddler to preschooler, as the happiest, most satisfying time of my life, in spite of the sadness of Brian's death, and the knotty, difficult reality of my marriage. Simply, my love for Reid sustained me. I continued to be fascinated by his development—each new stage was infinitely interesting and surprising.

Every step of his coming into consciousness seemed a miracle. One morning, when he was not quite eight months, he and I were at the kitchen table as Keith was leaving for work. Reid sat in a little plastic yellow seat that hooked under the table; his chubby legs, in his terry pajama suit with feet, kicked with pleasure as I fed him his breakfast. "Daddy's leaving for work," I told him, glancing over at the door. "Bye-bye, Keith," I said, idiotically. I waved at him and turned back to Reid to give him another spoonful. But Reid, a wet paste of cereal dribbling from his chin, clutched the arms of his seat and twisted around awkwardly to see his father. Then he lifted up one sticky hand. "Oh my God," I whispered as he opened and closed it a couple of times, scraping the air with his fingers.

I rode on the high of moments like that for days. It seemed the only truly important thing in the world to me then, to help along and to chronicle our son's discovery of the world.

Besides, it was fun. In contrast to the way that my life with Keith often felt closed, and then, after Brian died, dark as well, when I was with our son I felt that nearly every moment was felicitous, with its own unchallengeable meaning. Being with him often provoked the feeling that I was seeing things for the first time: pushing him in his stroller through the park on a warm day fragrant with spring, while he slept contentedly, hands folded in his lap and his face turned up like a new flower toward the sun;

riding the ferry to Staten Island, getting on my knees to peer down with him at the black, choppy water that through the metal mesh rail looked as wide as the sea; exploring the narrow back-streets of the city on my bicycle, with Reid chattering at me amiably from the molded child seat screwed onto the wheel be-hind—during all of these times I remember thinking, I have never been happier in my life.

Reid's development was one of the few things outside his work-related interests that Keith took pleasure in, so noticing it, talking about it, became one of the ways he and I continued to connect.

The power of the love and admiration Keith and I shared for Reid astonished me; I knew that it wasn't enough to keep us together, and I suppose we would have shared it even if we had not stayed together, but for me it worked as an incentive, moti-vating me to find a way to be with Keith and with Reid, which would allow the three of us to appreciate it. I believed that one of the benefits of my staying with Keith was that it gave Reid a better chance of having a strong relationship with his father. I knew that the more time Keith spent with him, the better he would understand what they might have together.

The highlights of this time—when Keith was in the early stages of his recovery—were never the holidays or the rare trips we took, but instead the most mundane, ordinary moments, when the three of us were just being together and there was no palpable tension or anger. That seemed miraculous. Reid, at two, seemed to pull us together magnetically.

"I want to eat Chinese food on the coffee table and watch TV like Daddy!" he declared one evening. He wore a one-piece red pajama suit with blue and yellow piping. The suit was tight across his middle where his round baby belly stretched it out over the snaps. He had just had a bath, and his hair was spiky and damp on the ends.

"Okay," I said, "but a kiss first." Reid lifted his arms and threw them around my neck. He was fragrant with baby soap.

After I got a good whiff, I put him down. "Seltzer, too, please," he said imperiously over his shoulder, as he waddled over to the couch. "Like Dad's," he added, with a wave of his hand.

Keith sat on the sofa and pulled the coffee table up so that he could eat. Reid wedged himself in between the table and the couch, and stood in front of his plate. Glancing over at Keith, he picked up his spoon with his fist and shoveled a great mound of fried rice into his mouth.

"This is the life, huh, Reidie?" Keith said. "Chinese food on the coffee table, TV, and everything."

"Yep, it's good all right," said Reid. He squashed some peas with a butter knife. A few little pieces of rice dropped from his lips as he talked. "It's delicious."

Keith rarely came home early enough to see Reid before I put him to bed; I cherished these moments when Reid had time with his father. It felt ordinary, conventional, uncomplicated. While I often felt with Keith as if I were inching my way along a tightrope, at times like this I felt as if I were walking on a wide, open road where I could relax my stride, take a breath, admire the view. "Wait," I said, "don't move. I'll be right back." I went for my camera.

These photos I have of Keith and Reid—eating fried rice together in the living room, or sharing a plate of chicken at a picnic table at a county fair, or sitting side-by-side at their desks, drawing quietly—these photos I took, I think, as a way to capture their relationship, hoping to make it stick.

When I watch the videos we took when Reid was small— some before Brian died and before Keith became addicted, and some afterward—I'm struck by how normal everything looks. There was no video the Christmas Keith was in rehab, of course, but even on Reid's third birthday, only a year after Keith left the hospital, Keith is there at the little party, looking a bit thin, still, but engaged. He's using the camera for most of the party, moving it slowly from close-ups of Reid's watchful face to his friends', then over to the mothers, standing around the table, chatting, cordial. He catches the eye of Reid's sitter, the young, pretty Bajan woman. She gazes back at him, into the camera; the camera moves away, then slyly back. She follows it with her eyes, and allows a shy smile. The camera moves away again, then back again, away, then mischievously back, until she's smiling broadly. It is Keith who is playing with her, Keith behind the camera, teasing.

"Who wants to take over?" says his disembodied voice. Then there is Keith, sitting on the floor, a couple of three-year-olds in fancy dress, cake-stained in a sugar-daze, milling around him as he fiddles with the controls on the video machine. I can see that he has come over to the party from work, because he is wearing dark trousers and a tailored shirt and elegant shoes. He's completely unselfconscious about being videoed. But he looks healthy—that's what I can't reconcile. There is in his face not a trace of the pain and the struggle I remember from that time. In my head I keep checking the dates (December of 1985, he was in the hospital, he got out in January 1986, this video was taken in February, the beginning of February 1987) because the way Keith looks contradicts everything that I remember feeling then. It's as if we were leading two lives: the life we shared with the world at large, and the life we shared with the other people we knew who were also "recovering." Seeing Keith in our videos helps me understand how our family and some of our friends did not know how serious our trouble was.

14

The spring after his slip, Keith began going to AA meetings in earnest. His meeting began around cocktail time, and lasted for an hour or more, so he would go right from work and not come home till nine o'clock or later. I was still spending my evenings alone with Reid, usually eating dinner by myself.

I believed Keith needed to go to meetings, but as the months of recovery rolled along, I began to view AA as yet another way for Keith to distance himself from me and from Reid. I sometimes felt resentful of the time he spent away from us, and suspicious about what he was doing there with these other recovering addicts and alcoholics. Keith and I, though our relationship was less fraught with crises, didn't seem to be getting any closer. On the rare nights when Keith did come home early enough to see Reid before I put him to bed, he spent most of the time on the telephone, talking with AA people. Though I could see that AA was helping Keith, I also wondered if he wasn't substituting one addiction for another.

One evening, when we had agreed that I would meet him for dinner after a meeting, I arrived just as the group was breaking up. It was a cool, fall night, and the dark street was damp and cluttered with fallen leaves that gave off a pungent, suburban smell. At the end of the block I could see a small knot of people, and then more, as they trickled out of a nearby brownstone, standing in the soft light that spilled from the doorway. There were men and women in business suits, and in jeans, and from a distance, they all looked young and interesting. A party crowd. Of course, I thought ironically as I approached, they're drug addicts and alcoholics, *just my type.* I spotted Keith. A woman had tapped him shyly on the shoulder and he turned around. I watched them in profile as she said something to him, and slowly they embraced. When they separated, they held hands for a moment, spoke again, and then she walked away.

From nowhere, a huge swell of rage seemed to pick me up and carry me toward Keith. I no longer wanted to meet him; I wanted to land on him. Hard. I thought I had never seen him as tender. His welcoming gestures with his AA friend suggested to me all the intimacy I longed for.

"Hi, Keith," I said coolly, "who's your friend?" I pointed with my chin toward the woman, who was now chatting with a group of people.

"That's Elaine," Keith said. "She's only got a couple of weeks."

"It looks like she'd like to have a couple of weeks with you."

Keith scowled at me. "Why do you say things like that?" he said. "You don't understand what this means to me."

"You're right," I said. "I don't understand." I walked ahead quickly. "Let's just get something to eat."

I was hungry, greedy for change. I could see that this AA thing was having some effect on Keith, and that was fine. But I wanted it to work for us.

Keith would often come home from a meeting (and sometimes another hour or so of coffee and chatting afterward) flushed with what I interpreted as a kind of self-satisfied vigor. I always wanted to know if he had spoken or "shared" in the meeting; I wondered whether he ever talked about us.

He did confess once that he had spoken about me. "I shared tonight that you saved my life," Keith told me one evening. I felt a moment of exhilaration: a public acknowledgment!

Then Keith looked at me sheepishly. He flapped his arms weakly at his sides. "And that I hated you for it," he said.

I paced around the kitchen counter, thinking. "You know, you're *really* starting to piss me off," I said.

"Well, but I didn't save your life," I continued defensively after a minute. "I helped you to make a choice." As I stood there thinking about it, I began to consider how important it was to draw the distinction. If Keith believed that I saved his life against his will, that I pulled him out of the turbulent waters of his self-destruction when he would have preferred to go down, I felt that his anger at me would have been justified. (Not pretty, but justified.) I thought back on the days when he seemed most determined to kill himself, and I saw myself taking care of his business, taking care of our son, helping Keith decide to get into treatment. But one of my most powerful feelings during that time was of a helplessness delivered of the understanding that I could not save Keith's life, that living was a choice he would have to make alone. It was terrifying, that helplessness, but also liberating. It allowed me to believe that no matter what happened to Keith, I would not be responsible.

Now, hearing him hand me that responsibility, with resentment, rather than offering an acknowledgment (and gratitude) that I had helped him, made me determined that both of us understood what had happened.

He spent hours on the phone with fellow AA members, murmuring, laughing, and—I was sure—revealing himself in ways that he would never reveal himself to me. I would sit in the next room trying to read, my fragile web of concentration suddenly snagged by a point in Keith's conversation. "The same is true for me . . ." I would hear, or "Whenever that happens to me, I . . ." and I'd find myself finally giving up on my book and staring up at the ceiling as I strained to hear what came next. Inevitably, Keith's stream of words would then drop to an undercurrent, too deep and too faint for me to follow.

Who were these people who called and left their first name only, like a lost glove, on our answering machine?

One of them began to call regularly and frequently; Keith spoke to me a little bit about how he felt Tony was helping him. Keith planned to ask Tony if he would act as his sponsor, a kind of personal guide through AA's program of recovery. They were often on the phone for hours. Tony had just broken up with his wife, I think, or was trying to sort out some other messy relationship, and I had the sense—possibly from snatches of conversation, or bits and pieces of the story Keith had told me—that they spent a lot of time discussing the difficulties they were having with women. Whether this was so or not, the idea made me feel both left out and antagonistic.

On the anniversary of Keith's first full year of sobriety, I joined him at his regular meeting. The room was hot and smoky and the lighting was bad; the pale cream stucco walls were scuffed and drab. I felt as if I were back in junior high school, in a friend's unfinished basement for a necking party. The only thing missing was a record player scratching out "Norwegian Wood." There was a large sheet cake with white frosting and frilly pink borders sitting on a card table in the far corner. For a moment I wondered if it was somebody's birthday, and then I remembered: this was a celebration. I stood against the wall and watched the easy intimacy among the group, the way the men and women asked after each other with kindness and with an eagerness that was sometimes so aggressive, I found it almost alarming. Several people slapped Keith on the back: "It's your anniversary, man?" and embraced him. Others slipped him congratulatory cards; one man shyly thrust him a small, foil-wrapped grocery store bouquet. I was fiddling with the buckle on my bag

and looking out over the room when Keith approached to intro-
duce me to someone.

"Val, this is Tony," he said.

"Oh my God," I said.

Though Tony was half a head taller than Keith, their resemblance was extraordinary. They looked like brothers, even twins.
"Don't you see it?" I asked. "Don't you see how much you look
alike?"

Both men looked at each other, and then expectantly back
at me.

"Oh, hello," I said, taking Tony's hand. I was surprised at
how friendly he was. When Keith moved away and left us talking, I found myself searching Tony's face, still astonished at the
resemblance, and also trying to connect this man to the man
Keith had been having his telephone conversations with. I don't
really know what I had expected, but Tony seemed like just another guy. Not especially messed up. Not diabolical. Ordinary. I
was both relieved and disappointed.

When the meeting was close to beginning, someone—an
older woman in a tweed suit and pearls, fussing importantly—
arranged four or five straight-backed chairs in the front of the
room, facing the group. The room seemed to get smaller by the
minute, shrinking and losing air as the size of the crowd increased. The chairs were jammed up against the wall, and when
the guests of honor—those celebrating anniversaries—were
seated, nervously gripping their cards or bouquets and facing the
packed room with what appeared to be a combination of expec-
tancy and excitement and fear, they looked as if they might have
been facing a firing squad. They each had a turn to say a few
words, remaining seated while they spoke since there was no
room to stand, and this, too, gave the impression that they were
trapped, bargaining for their lives, or at least making a case for
themselves. I grew nervous as Keith's turn came; he normally

spoke so softly, I wondered how anyone would hear him. He began, "My name is Keith and I'm an addict . . ." and he spoke so deliberately and with such forced confidence that I knew that he had thought hard about what he was going to say and had rehearsed it. He pushed a strand of hair away from his eyes when he'd finished talking and threw a brief, unfocused glance my way. I barely had time to catch it, and no chance to respond. I guess I wanted to give him a look of encouragement or appreciation or support or something, but I found that I was judging him, in spite of myself, wishing that he'd been more eloquent, funnier. And also feeling slightly stung that he hadn't said something about me. Something specific, in fact. Though I couldn't admit it then, what I wished Keith had said was, "You've all been great, but if it weren't for my wife, I might not be here today. I want to thank her for her love and support." A light spattering of applause would have been nice.

But, of course, Keith didn't feel that way.

After the meeting, we straggled over to a nearby diner with a group of Keith's friends. I think it was the first time in my adult life that I'd gone out with anyone for dinner—certainly not with a group this large—when no one ordered a drink. It was the kind of place where they serve tart red wine that throws off a rusty smell and suedes up your tongue, but I was tempted, anyway. Everyone ordered Coke or coffee; the fact that they weren't drinking made them seem vulnerable to me, as if they had no choice but to be open about their problem. Though their talk was constant, and punctuated with laughter, as I gazed over the gray Formica table littered with overflowing ashtrays, half-eaten sandwiches, and coffee and soft drinks going cold and flat, I thought they were a sad-looking group.

Everything about their engagement seemed forced and strained; their conversation seemed to have no life, as if it were a reluctant engine that whined to a coughing start only to splutter

and stall and have to be coaxed with a grinding whine into starting all over again. I found myself staring distractedly into the
smoky, veined mirror behind our booth at a stranger, ghostly in
the reflection, dark, and remote. It was only when I saw him
suddenly throw back his head and I heard a familiar staccato
laugh that I realized with astonishment that the face I had been
staring at was Keith's.

One of the basic Al-Anon precepts is that it is a bad idea—
a bad choice—to remain in a relationship because you hope or
believe that your partner will change. I was very strict with myself about being aware that I was making the choice to stay with
Keith, despite our conflicts. I didn't want to look back at our
marriage fifteen or twenty years down the road and think, I
should have stabbed him in his sleep, or to think that I had
endured the marriage for that long, sustained only by the hope
that one day it would be better. It seemed to me then that it
would have been very easy to do that. There were compelling
reasons to stay: he's suffered terribly, he needs me; we have a
child, who needs us. But I knew that those reasons weren't in
themselves powerful enough to keep me there if I were miserable. And so every day I reminded myself that I had to make a
choice; every day I knew I had to feel comfortable with that
choice.

A *difficult* marriage. "My marriage was difficult, too," a
friend confided to me once; it was the first time that I had ever
thought of my own marriage that way. Though my friend's statement had made me sad (why could I not be in an easy marriage?), it also had the odd effect of making me feel optimistic:
difficult, I could handle. I wouldn't leave my marriage just because it was difficult.

But inherent in having to make a daily choice was the

haunting idea that I had made a mistake. I couldn't imagine that marriage was this hard for everyone. It would have helped me to understand then that what Keith and I were going through was, essentially, a phase (albeit a long and arduous one), and that once we were past it, living together would be altogether different, because we would be different. Our marriage was full of conflict because we were changing, both of us, and so every day seemed to present some struggle or another. I remember often thinking to myself, This is just too much fucking work.

Yet often, too, I felt comfort in the familiarity of my routines, and in the feeling I seemed to be stuck on: this marriage isn't yet what it's going to be. I didn't feel sure enough of myself to know exactly what it was I wanted; when I did, then I figured that would be the time to evaluate whether or not I would remain married to Keith. In the meantime, I tried to put away my balance sheet. Was I working harder than Keith? Had I given more to the relationship than he? When I was angry at him, that was the ledger I went to, where I could leaf through and count up the cumulative ways I had been better than he, more generous, more honest, healthier. I would go to him, my resentments fresh off the page, and say, "Look what I've done for you! Why don't you appreciate everything I've done?" and Keith would look at me as if I were from another planet. "Why don't you do something for yourself?" he'd say. And I'd run off to an Al-Anon meeting in a huff, where I'd hold up my ledger and someone would say, "I know exactly how you feel. But he may not be ready to tell you he appreciates you. He may never be. Now keep the focus on yourself."

"Just for today," I'd fume, *"just for today,"* and I'd put my ledger away.

I must have been about six when I first asked my mother, "How will I know when I fall in love?"

"You'll know," she told me. Her tone was solemn, reassuring. Thinking back on that from the perspective of my marriage, I had come to the conclusion that either my mother had no idea what she was talking about, or I was missing out on one of the great secrets of life.

Either way I looked at it, it was disappointing.

"If I stay with him, he's going to have to change," I said to Keith's office manager one evening early on in Keith's recovery. We were sitting at the kitchen table, sipping Pernod and discussing, among other things, what was happening with Keith's business.

"People don't change," Robert said.

"We'll see," I had said. But I knew then that I was changing, and if Keith and I were to be together, he would have to, too.

15

Because of the work I continued to do in therapy as a result of my parent-dream, all my relationships were different. If I had thought I was seeing the real world for the first time when I discovered through Al-Anon an ability to maintain my equilibrium in a relationship, then I now was discovering how to progress from that point. Once I discarded my need to be second best, I felt at once less afraid and more alive, more able to make choices that satisfied me.

The spring Reid was two, I had finished the book I was working on and begun freelancing for magazines again. I knew I didn't yet want to take a full-time job; I enjoyed being with our son too much to consider it seriously, and financially Keith and I could manage on what he was earning from his business.

As a way to give us something to do a couple of mornings a week, I enrolled Reid in a music class for toddlers. There was another mother there, Lou, with two young boys just over a year apart, who intrigued me. She was a big woman with perfect, rosy English skin; she was unselfconsciously stylish, in loose jumpsuits and beautiful scarves and her long dark hair in a thick braid down her back. Occasionally she left the class to pull a cellular phone from the recesses of her black leather backpack. When she saw me eyeing her one day as she prepared to make a call, the look on my face must have betrayed what I thought of making calls from Music and Movement for Two's and Three's. "I'm sorry," she said, sincerely, "I know what you must be thinking. You're right, it's disgusting, but it's the lesser of two evils for me right now. Would you and Reid like to come to David's birthday

party next week?" She said this all in one breath, straightfor-
wardly, as if she were hurriedly dealing out a deck of cards.

We went, and the boys dove into their own world instantly
(partly, I think, because Lou's six foot three husband, dressed up
for the occasion in a polka-dotted clown suit and garish makeup,
terrified Reid and some of the other kids), and Lou and I made a
date to get together the following week in the park with the
children. After the first few hours of our conversation that day as
we roamed the grassy hills and playgrounds of Central Park following our boys, I began to feel with certainty that I had met
someone remarkable. Over the course of more afternoons in the
park and dinners out, just the two of us, Lou revealed—not all at
once, but in modest increments—that she had recently moved to
New York from Toronto because her husband's job had been
temporarily transferred here, that she'd been married once before, that she had traveled around the world, lived overseas,
trekked in the Himalayas, graduated from (a prestigious, I found
out later) law school, had been one of the three women who
drafted Canada's Equal Rights Amendment and led the fight to
ratify it. (It was ratified.) The tiny white enamel pin she wore on
her lapel, often covered by a diaper she had thrown over her
shoulder or the sleeping head of one of her boys, was the symbol
of her induction into the Order of Canada.

I knew that a year ago I would have been too intimidated
by this woman to have pursued a friendship. Now I waded in, a
bit at a time, casting off my fears about not being good enough,
smart enough, clever enough, like clothes that would encumber a
swim. We discussed our children, our work, our marriages, our
therapy, our feelings about ourselves and each other. I had never
had a friendship like this before, as intimate and intense, or as
open. I was astonished by Lou's insights into my behavior—and
just as astonished by my insights into hers. The friendship had
the effect of taking pressure off my relationship with Keith, as

well as giving me a different perspective on it. Often, in hearing Lou's responses to my conflicts with Keith, I felt more sure of my own responses. In my relationship with Lou I had found another way to use what I had been learning and to feel the effects of my progress. Our friendship continued to deepen, we both felt enriched, we loved and we treasured one another.

Though they were not as intimate, my other friendships deepened, too. I was offered and accepted a part-time job as a magazine editor. The freelance writing assignments I took on were fun. I felt both a competent and playful mother. And more and more often I would have one of those moments with Keith, when he knew exactly what I was feeling even before I did and he understood, or he'd read a story I'd be working on and say, "This is really good, but here, wouldn't it be more honest to say . . ." and he'd be right. He was reading *The Hobbit* to Reid, using funny voices for the different characters and relishing Reid's absorption, wrapping his son snugly under one arm while he turned the pages with his other hand. "Just one more page!" Reid would plead when it was time for bed, and Keith would always acquiesce. The tenderness with which he carried his son to bed, the way he caressed Reid's face as he leaned over him to kiss him good-night, all of these things moved me to think, I am so glad I've stuck this out.

One evening after work Keith walked in with a large white box from Saks, wrapped in a ridiculously huge bow. He presented it to me and kissed me on the cheek. "Open it," he said. I felt silly; it wasn't my birthday, or any special day, and that bow was so . . . big. Inside, a beautiful, soft lambskin jacket lay nestled in pink tissue paper. There was a card in the pocket. "Dear Val," it read, "A token of my esteem. A mere token. I love you, Keith."

We had decided that we had enough money to rent a small house again in the country for the summer. Keith read all the ads and made the phone calls; his persistence and determination, his confidence about what he wanted, and his easy way with the people who answered his calls made me feel happy, taken care of. We looked at a few houses; there was something about making a decision together that seemed to unite us. We both knew what we were looking for. One of the houses, a pretty stone cottage set back from a glassy pond, might have suited us fine. But as the owner sat at a picnic table in the yard, telling us about the charms of the place (his house was on the same property), he slowly finished off a bottle of Chardonnay. It was ten o'clock in the morning. Keith and I didn't even need to look at each other. We thanked him and told him we'd call with our decision. Back in the car, we exchanged a glance and shuddered. As we drove away, down a dirt road under a thick canopy of trees, I put my hand over Keith's as it lay on the front seat between us. He looked at me and smiled. "Onward," he said.

"I think you make the turn here," I said as we drove toward a stand of pines. Keith leaned forward into the steering wheel and squinted at the handmade road sign.

"This is it," he said. "Dapler Lane." We turned onto a long gravel driveway and rolled, the tires crunching deliciously, to the end. A bungalow came into view behind a towering pile of firewood.

"Hmmmm, modest," I said.

Getting out of the car and walking toward the house, we could see a glimpse of a lake, dark and sparkling in the bright sun. A screen door slammed in the house next door and a white-haired man in chinos and T-shirt doddered out with a wide smile, his hand extended for a shake.

"You must be the Monroes!" he said broadly, drawing out the name as if we were a family of twelve. An ancient beagle shuffled over to Reid and began lackadaisically nosing his sneakers. "I'm Harold. Very glad to meet you." We shook hands and followed him inside the little house.

"Lil—my wife—and I, we built all this ourselves," Harold said. "Our house, too." The bungalow was tiny—not much bigger than our living room at home—spotlessly clean, and furnished with a secondhand sofa and chairs. There were glass doors opening onto a deck, which overlooked a lawn that rolled gently down to the lake. A swing set, slightly rusted, stood off to the side. The lawn was immaculately well-kept.

Down at the dock, Harold showed us the battered old rowboat ("a seasoned little boat," I think Harold said) and pointed out that the shallow beach, carpeted with pebbles, would be a fine place for Reid, then four, to become accustomed to the water. We agreed. We stood on the dock inhaling the March air. Maybe we needed to think about it, Harold suggested. Would we like to take the rowboat out on the lake and think about it?

We strapped a life jacket around Reid, who was as excited by the adventure as if we were sailing to India, and rowed out into the lake. Keith struggled against a stiff wind. As I watched him, I remembered an afternoon the summer before we were married, when we drove up to a lake not far from this one, had a picnic, and decided to rent a boat. We got about fifty feet from the shore when Keith, who was finding the oars unwieldy anyway, suddenly became unable to lift either one of them out of the water. Other boaters drifted by peacefully, languid and happy in the heat.

"What's the matter, honey?" I asked. "Are they too heavy for you?"

Rivulets of sweat slid down the sides of Keith's face. "I can't get these fucking things out of the fucking water!" he said.

The boat rocked as he tried pulling one oar and then the other toward him. "Goddamit!" he said, standing up and leaning, with all his weight, on an oar. It came flying up into the air, dragging a stream of water and an enormous clot of slimy green weeds. Clutching the sides of the boat, I leaned back and let out one of those hair-raising, tongue-waving, tonsil-popping horror movie screams, which alarmed Keith, who let go of the oar as if it were hot-wired in the water, and fell back down heavily opposite me. He wiped his forehead with the back of his arm.

"What was that?" he said. I raised my eyebrows at him.

"Let's get out of here," I said, glancing around at the other boaters, who all were beginning to look as if they belonged to some sort of demonic local cult. Laughing at ourselves, we poked our way back to shore.

Now we sat in a chilly wind in the middle of another lake, Reid between us, and looked around. The sun was just beginning to go down, and on the surrounding hills the trees, still bare from winter, scratched black branches against a whitening sky. The water was dark and luminous, like opal. Keith and I looked at each other and nodded.

"Definitely," I said. "Let me have the oars; I want to row back."

When we got to the dock, as Reid fiddled with his life jacket, Keith and I hugged. "It's so beautiful, isn't it," we said. "It's just what we've been looking for."

That was the summer Keith made formal amends to the people he knew he'd hurt. Following the ninth step of the AA program, he set about to "make direct amends . . . wherever possible . . ." My turn came on a tranquil, sunny morning as I sat sipping coffee on a white metal chair on the deck of our little house. Far away, a buzz saw droned lazily, then stopped, then droned again. Keith came up behind me, bent down, and whispered in my ear, "I have some things I need to say to you."

The sky always seemed to be a vivid blue that summer—or at least on weekends, when we were at the lake—and the two of us seemed to have spent an impossible amount of time, considering that Reid was a lively four-year-old, just sitting around staring up at it through the lacy, verdurous veil of the treetops.

I took a swig of my coffee, hooked my toes under the smooth lip of another chair, and pulled it around to face me. "Be my guest," I said.

I'm yearning to write here that Keith begged my forgiveness and told me that he would spend the rest of his life making it all up to me. No one would know the difference. Keith can't remember what he said, and the truth is, neither can I. But I remember the form of it; I can see Keith before me now, serious and intentional, and the words he is speaking are a meticulously designed statement, all straight lines and right angles, in black and white. They had all the charm of a fax, but they were delivered efficiently.

Though neither of us remember his words, we both recall how I responded to him when he was through. I had been toying with my sunglasses, and now I put them down on the table beside me. "That's the first time I've ever heard you take responsibility for what you've done," I said. But there was so much more I'd wanted him to say.

God, I was thinking, we have a long way to go.

I continued to go to Al-Anon, and Keith to AA, and though our relationship had stabilized, we didn't seem to be getting anywhere fast. Whatever our problem was sometimes seemed too complicated for those programs, or we didn't know how to apply what we heard there to help ourselves. Often, after a long stretch of silence and a general secession of Keith from the relationship, I would say, *Enough, either things change or we separate.* Then Keith would come to, as if coming out of a sleep, and promise me that he would try to accommodate my needs and be more present. In my own mind, and to several of my friends, I would say that I'd give it till May, or October, or February, and if things hadn't changed by then, I would negotiate a separation. In the meantime I would step back, spending more time than usual with my friends, not bothering to include Keith in my plans. With the distance I had initiated between us, Keith found it easier to approach me. It would usually take a couple of months for us to work our way back to our original stance, with me at the line, demanding Keith toe it, and Keith backing off, telling me, no way. So it went on like this for two years or more.

Often I thought, it takes two to do the dance we do; if I stop dancing he'll have to, too. Or else he'll have to make up some new steps. All right, then, let's see what happens if I don't go away after I tell him what I want. I'll just say what I feel and stand there.

But what if I cry?

What if he walks?

We seemed to be traveling on parallel paths, close enough to touch as we moved along, but never intersecting.

"I don't know about you and me," Keith said when I described our parallel closeness and told him I felt frustrated by it, "but that pretty much describes the relationship I had with Brian.

"As kids, we were always with one another, and we had a kind of comfortable closeness derived from that.

"But intimate? No, we weren't intimate, the way you would like us to be."

I thought again about what it would be like to have another person around all of the time, someone who so looked and acted like me that people often mistook us for one another . . . and the effect of that on my sense of boundaries, who I was, what I chose to reveal about myself, and what I chose to share.

Keith's silences and his need for separateness, once opaque, seemed to be becoming clearer to me, cleaner and more transparent, as if I could see through them into the works inside his head.

"Keith," I said, one night after dinner, "I think I'm lonely." I thought I could see the slow tide of terror rising into his eyes.

"But I can't keep you from being lonely. You have to get a feeling of wholeness, of completeness from inside yourself."

"I know that," I said. "But that's not what I'm talking about. I'm not talking about cosmic loneliness; I'm talking about cleaning-up-after-dinner loneliness, no-phone-call-in-the-middle-of-the-day loneliness, nobody-there-to-laugh-at-my-joke loneliness.

"After all we've been through together, I wish we could be friends."

Keith was characteristically quiet. Then he said, "Me, too."

"What can we do about it?"

"I'm not sure," he said. He looked at me and sighed. Then he reached across the table and took my hand. "Sometimes I think you want me to be someone else," Keith said.

"No, no!" I told him. "I only want you to be more yourself!"

"Come with me, honey," he said after a minute, rising from his chair, making Groucho eyebrows and leading me toward the bedroom. "I want to share a little more of myself with you right now."

On a spectacular spring morning, Keith suggested we take Reid, then about six, up to the park. I, who exercised every day and was rarely sick, could only say that I felt weird, I didn't know if I should go. "Come on," Keith said, "it's a beautiful day. Being outside'll make you feel better."

I thought he might be right. But as I sat on a park bench in the sunshine, I felt sicker and sicker, as if some poison were working on me. I motioned to Keith, who was playing catch with Reid. He said something to Reid and came over to me. "I need to go home," I said. "I'm feeling really bad." When I tried to get up, I was stiff as an old dog. I could hardly straighten my arms or legs. A flat rash that started on my neck crept down the insides of my arms to the palms of my hands. Later, at home, I saw that the rash covered my body, and the soles of my feet. My hands and my feet itched wildly.

The next day Keith fixed Reid breakfast and took him to school, while I saw a doctor who had my blood tested for everything he could think of: Lyme, autoimmune disorders, hepatitis. Nothing came up positive. When after about a week the symptoms had pretty much disappeared but had left me weak and shaking, I made an appointment with a neurologist, fantasizing about having some kind of degenerative disease. I called Keith at the studio to ask if he would come with me.

"Why do you need me to come?" he said impatiently. "It's probably nothing. We'll be sitting in the doctor's office for hours. I'm completely overwhelmed with work."

"Forget it. I'll go with a friend."

"It's nothing, Val. I'm sure you're fine. Why do you need me?"

"Because I do," I said. "I do need you, and you can't be there for me, and you know what? It fucking sucks." I hung up.

Keith phoned me back. "I'm coming with you," he said. "We'll talk about it later."

That night, after the appointment—at which the doctor allayed my fears—Keith sat down next to me in the living room. "I couldn't admit that there might be something seriously wrong with you," he said. "That's why I kept telling you I thought you were fine. I did think you were fine.

"But I also couldn't face the idea that I might lose you the way I lost Brian." Keith reached for me and then stopped. He looked away. "I just don't think I could stand that," he said.

"But I *needed* you, for Christ's sake," I said angrily. "I needed you to put your own stuff aside and be with me. Why can't you do that? Why won't you? It just isn't acceptable that you don't!" I had begun to cry.

"I'm trying," Keith said. "I am, Val. I am."

"Well try fucking harder," I said.

As I began to feel better and gain strength back, our routines at home took on some normalcy, and there were days when I felt as if we actually lived like a typical family, which at that point was beginning to seem to me like a step in the right direction.

"Elevator's here!" called Reid as Keith and I rushed to get ready to get to work. Usually I would drop Reid off at school and then head uptown. Keith and I grabbed for our coats as Reid held the "open door" button.

"Come on, come on!" he called impatiently in his high voice from inside the elevator. "My finger's getting tired!"

We rushed in. "Whew!" Reid said, shaking his hand to get the blood back as the door clanked closed. "What took you two?"

Keith was standing opposite me. "Look at your mother," he said to Reid. Keith looked at me appreciatively.

"Yeah," said Reid, glancing me over. "So?"

"So? So?" said Keith. Suddenly he did a joyful little jump, grabbed me around the waist, and lifted me off the floor. I dropped my briefcase. "She's wonderful!" he cried. "And she's mine, all mine!" He conjured a deep, wicked laugh, and kissed me all over my neck.

I kissed him back. He put me down and I took a step away, partly to steady myself, partly because I was unaccustomed to such a display from Keith. "What's got into you?" I said, but I felt glad.

"I don't know," Keith said as we reached the lobby. "Maybe I'm in love."

"I hope this time it's with me," I said.

"I'd like to go to South Carolina to the retreat for a long weekend," Keith said a couple of months later as we were getting ready for bed. "Do you want to come?"

I didn't.

"I could take Reid," Keith said. "I think it would be fun to be down there, just the two of us together."

The idea both delighted and scared me. Reid and I had never spent more than a day apart. I knew that he would be fine without me, but could Keith really take care of him? He had been clean for several years; I had no fear that he would slip. But I had been doing practically everything for Reid myself ever since he was born. How would Keith manage? Would he keep a close eye on him? Make sure that he was safe? Remember to feed him? Of course Reid announced loudly when he was hungry, and had already developed a pretty good sense of his own safety. I was no longer alerted by that long, ominous rumble of a chair being slowly dragged across the room, signaling that he was about to climb to a countertop for something out of his reach. I thought about the prospect of an entire weekend at home, alone. It was thrilling.

I looked into the suitcase one last time before I shut it. Seeing Reid's things tucked in neatly next to Keith's made me think of the two of them together. I had always thought of Reid as my son, or our son; never Keith's son. Thinking about the potential of their relationship gave me a whole other perspective on both of them. Keith as father, Reid as Keith's son. They inhabited another world apart from mine. I want them both to flourish there, I thought, as I snapped the metal closures. I think it was the first time I fully allowed myself to wish that for them.

I went downstairs to wait with Reid while Keith ran out to get a cab to take them to the airport. It was early morning; a weak yellow light leaked into the narrow corridor of our empty street.

"He's here!" Reid cried eagerly, pushing open the lobby door when Keith pulled up in the cab.

"Have a great time," I told them both, hugging Reid first, and then Keith. "I love you."

"Love you, too, Mom!" Reid said as I shut the cab door. I took a few steps back to the curb as the taxi pulled away. Reid turned around to look at me, his face small and low in the cab's broad back window. Keith turned, too, and put his hand on Reid's back. They both smiled and waved, looking pleased.

Back upstairs, the house was still. As I got ready for work, I began to luxuriate in the quiet. After I showered, I took my coffee over to the couch and stretched out, thinking about how I would spend the weekend. For the three days ahead, I had no responsibilities; no one to take care of but myself.

As I left the house that morning I thought, it doesn't matter what time I come back, I can stay out as late as I like, and eat whatever and whenever I like and do whatever I like. The feeling of freedom increased as I walked, and I moved faster and faster as if I were running to catch the time, as if it would slip away.

"Hi, Mom!" Reid's voice chimed small and clear over the telephone.

"How are you, sweetie? Are you having a good time?"

"Sure," Reid said. "Here's Dad."

There was a moment of dead wire while Reid held the phone out for his father.

"Hi, hon," Keith said as he picked it up.

"How're you doing?"

"Really well. I'm tired, but we're doing fine. And you?"

I flashed over the movies and the meals and the long bike rides I had taken. "I'm having a great time," I said.

"We miss you," said Keith.

"Likewise," I said. "See you Sunday." I tried to imagine my husband and son hanging out together; though I could see them in my mind's eye, their conversation, their connection, was closed to me. They hadn't ever spent much time together before this—at least, not time concentrated in this way—so I had no template of what it would be like for them.

They returned companionable, tired and tan. Glancing into their suitcase as Keith unpacked, I noticed that Reid's clothes were almost exactly as they were when they'd left.

"Didn't he wear any of the things I packed?" I asked Keith.

"Oh, I guess not," Keith said.

Later that night as I was getting Reid ready for bed, we talked about the trip. "I was just wondering," I said, "did Daddy ever give you a shower this weekend?"

Reid thought a moment. "Nope," he said, finally. "No showers!" He grinned happily at the idea. Three days was definitely the longest my son had ever been without a shower or bath. He probably didn't brush his teeth, either. But he looked so fine and well in spite of it! I guessed he could spend time alone with his father and survive.

Once I was resigned to the idea that Keith believed angels controlled the weather, it wasn't much of a shock to find out that he also believed in ghosts. Those were the souls who, as I understood it, had accumulated more sanskaras than they'd worked off, and so they became stuck in a kind of prison (or an interminable layover) between spiritual planes. My attitude about Keith's devotion to Baba had become more relaxed; I loved what Meher Baba stood for, and its effect on Keith. His devotion seemed to give him peace. I'd have no problem with Baba at all, I figured, if only he hadn't told people he was God.

Reid naturally began to absorb some of Keith's beliefs—that Baba was God, and that it was good to honor him, but I never fully understood what Reid felt until one evening when we were sitting on his bed talking, just before I was about to turn out the lights. Keith had hung a framed black and white photo of Baba on the wall near Reid's bed, and though I looked at it sometimes as I settled Reid down for the night, I hadn't observed that it meant much to him.

But this evening, Reid turned to the photograph and looked at it tearfully.

"What is it, hon?" I asked, leaning toward him a bit.

Reid pointed toward the picture with one hand and wiped his tears, now falling fast, with the other.

"Oh, honey," I said. I put my arm around him. "Why are you crying?"

Reid shook his head.

"You don't know?"

"I'm not sure," he said.

"Are you sad?"

Reid shook his head.

"Well, then, are you relieved about something? Something we've been talking about?"

"No, not relieved," Reid said.

"Are you happy?" I said. "Sometimes we cry when we're happy, or moved, like how I cry at parades."

Reid stuck out his tongue and tasted his tears.

"Oh, I know what it is," he said softly. He sounded confident, resolved, and satisfied. He turned from the picture of Baba to look at me; he looked me right in the eye. Touching his finger to his cheek as if to point to his emotion, he said, "Mom, these are tears of love."

16

Traveling with Keith and Reid to visit Keith's family had, in the years of Keith's recovery, begun to make me appreciate that we were becoming a real family, the three of us. We had our own history; I knew Keith better than his own family did. On these trips, as I talked with Keith's sister or his father and stepmother, I often came across more slivers of information that helped me better understand who he was.

Keith's sister, Maggie, dicing onions in her small, neat kitchen in Oakland, stood back from the cutting board, squeezed her eyes shut for a second, and took a deep breath. "Whooo!" she said. "Burns!"

Wiping her eyes, she turned to face me. "At the time, I had no idea," she said, "that Brian had a problem with drugs." It was more than seven years since Brian's death.

Of the three siblings, Maggie was the most outgoing, the friendliest, the most socially engaged. Though she was four years the twins' junior, in all of the photographs I had seen of her with her brothers, she almost always nearly matched them in size. As an adult, she was as big as the boys, but graceful, and so boisterous and funny, it was hard to imagine that the three had all come from the same family. Both she and Keith told me that the boys used to tease her terribly, that they were terribly jealous of her, the girl, the baby, the baby born just one.

"Mom said her pregnancy with the twins was hard," Maggie told me. "She worked as a bank teller, and was on her feet all day.

"And the babies were premature. I remember Mom telling me that she thought they were ugly. Both babies had colic, so they always seemed to be crying, and they were on separate feeding schedules, so she never seemed to have a break.

"Dad was working a lot then, so Mom was most often alone with the kids. I don't think she ever had much help. God, it must have been hard for her," Maggie said. "Imagine having to take care of two difficult infants by yourself.

"She said that the babies' doctor told her just to put them in a room and shut the door when they cried." Thinking of her own one-year-old daughter, Maggie let out a heavy sigh. "How could anyone do that?" she said.

"You know, I think that difficult beginning permeated the rest of their childhood.

"I was the second child," Maggie said (though she was actually the third). "It was different for me. I was a girl, I was healthy and cute," she said. "I loved the boys, but they were very hard on me." She sat down at her kitchen table and leaned her head on her hand.

"You know what people always used to ask them?" Maggie said. "People would always say, 'Oh, you're twins! Well, who's older?' "

Because Keith was born first, he became the older brother. "I think eventually Brian perceived himself as second best," Maggie says.

Though the boys had separate bedrooms for most of the time they were growing up, Keith's room was larger, better, more well-appointed. "Brian's room was so small and so spare," Maggie remembered, "so devoid of any decoration or character, that we all used to call it 'the monk's room.' "

The first time Maggie visited us at home after Keith and I were married, she was working at a dance studio, and when I remarked on how strong she looked, she glanced mischievously at Keith. Flexing her arm muscles, she bet she could easily carry him around the living room. "Get out of here," Keith said, laughing nervously as he backed away. "No, no, really," Maggie said, and lunged. She was too quick for Keith. Picking him up around the waist, she marched him gallantly once around the rug. I don't think she was even winded.

But for all of her physical strength and bravado, she bent easily under Keith's strong words. I thought she admired him, and wanted him to think well of her.

"Brian was very hard to get to know," Maggie told me as she continued to prepare dinner that afternoon in Oakland. "He seemed to be more outgoing than Keith, but he kept a lot to himself.

"There were times when I felt that my nature, something about me, bugged Brian," Maggie said. "Maybe he loved me, but I don't think he liked me."

She stopped her chopping abruptly and put down the knife. "You know what he said to me the last time I saw him? It was really weird. But now I think he was trying to tell me that he had tried to hurt himself.

"It was about a month before he died. He asked me if I would take some stitches out of his head. He told me that he'd been in an accident, that he'd crashed the car. I told him, 'Brian, you have to be *careful,'* but it didn't occur to me then that he might have crashed the car deliberately.

"Anyhow, there I was, rooting around in his hair, looking for these stitches . . ."

"Did you actually take them *out?"* I asked, incredulous.

"It seems weird, now, doesn't it?" Maggie said. "I don't know why it didn't then. But no, I didn't take them out, they weren't ready to come out, and so I just didn't pursue it."

She was silent. I couldn't tell whether or not she was about to cry.

"I think he wanted me to know," she said softly. "I think he was asking me for help."

In one photograph taken of Keith's mother not very long before she died, she sits in a recliner in what looks like a family room, a patchwork afghan tucked over her belly, bloated with cancer. Though she's smiling, there's something unfocused about her face; she's still beautiful, but under her auburn wig her features are smudged. The cancer has eaten away at her glamorous edge. One of the twins, I can't tell which, sits on the arm of the chair and leans toward her, but not enough to touch. He is in his twenties, hair to his shoulders. When I think of this picture and I see the young man with his head cocked defiantly, chin up, I think it is Brian. Then, in my mind's eye, I see the picture again; this time, the man looks acquiescent. Then I'm sure it's Keith.

Keith and Maggie were at their mother's hospital bedside when she died. Their father had left town for a quick overnight business trip—the doctors had told him that his wife's condition wasn't likely to change and that he should go. She went into a coma while he was away.

"I can't remember where Brian was," Maggie says now. "Keith and I were there alone."

Keith remembers his father's howl as they met in the hospital corridor.

Thirteen years later, another funeral. This time, Keith's father sat crumpled in a straight-backed wooden chair. He had just seen Brian's body. I walked over to him and put my hand on his shoulder. He felt small under the jacket of his smart gray suit, like a child. "How're you doing, Jim," I said.

He looked up at me blankly for a second and seemed to startle when he recognized me. Then he started to cry. He covered his eyes with one hand. "He's so beautiful, Val," he said, crying. "He just looks so beautiful and so peaceful." I wanted him not to cry. I wanted him to do his crying privately, and present a dignified, composed face to the family. I was frightened by his sorrow, and ungracious. "I'm so sorry, Jim," I said, touching him while taking a step away. Except for Keith, I had never seen a man cry. It was unbearably distressing. I had to leave.

"Jim didn't talk about his grief over Brian for three years," Keith's stepmother, Sharon, told me. "He'd come home from the supermarket crying, and I'd run over to him saying, 'What's wrong? What's happened?' and he'd tell me, 'Nothing, nothing, I was only thinking.'

"Eventually he began to mention it when we were out socially," Sharon continued. "Someone would bring up the fact that he or she had lost a child, or knew someone who did, and Jim would admit that he had, too."

On a visit to their home in South Carolina a few years ago, I asked my father-in-law if he often thought about Brian.

"I believe what people need to do is to put their grief out of their mind," Keith's father told me as he sat on the end of a chaise by his pool. "That's the only way to do it. You can't dwell on it, because it makes you crazy. You have to move on. I had to stop thinking about Brian and Jean because if I continued, I thought I would just . . . I don't know, I would just . . ." He ran his hand over his head and looked at the ground. "Fall apart, I guess." A warm wind sent a shiver of ripples across the surface of the water.

"Sometimes I sit in the living room and look at that picture of Brian on the bookshelf," Jim said sadly. "And all I can think is, what a waste."

I was wondering, but wouldn't ask, do you feel guilty, Jim? Do you ever think you might have saved him? That you might have done something differently that could have helped Brian toward a different outlet for his pain?

Jim shifted uncomfortably.

"Is it too warm for you out here?" I asked.

"I'm fine," Jim said. "The thing is," he said, "the thing is, I wonder, if a person is born with a proclivity for addiction, might there be something that happens in childhood that touches it off?"

"I don't know; I don't think so," I said. I remembered that Sharon had told me that Jim thought he had been too hard on his kids.

"Did I ever tell you about what the boys did when they competed?" Jim suddenly asked. "I always thought this was interesting: when it was clear that one of them was better than the other at something, or that one of them was hands down going to beat the other, the one who was losing would drop out. Always. Just quit."

The air was tropical, and I was hot where we sat in the sun, but at that moment I got a chill that fluttered its way up my spine and lifted me with a shudder off my chair.

"Did Brian quit more than Keith?" I asked Jim.

He looked up at me, shading his eyes from the glare. "That wasn't something I noticed," he said.

I thought of Keith's successes with his business before Brian died, our marriage, our child—we had all of the outward appearances of happiness.

Had Brian quit?

"Jim said he thought he favored Keith," Sharon had told me over lunch on that same trip.

"The last time we saw Brian was when he came to visit us the winter before he died," Sharon remembered. "As Brian was leaving, he hugged me and said, 'Take care of Dad,'" Sharon said. "I had one of those flickers of feeling, you know what I mean? That you sense but ignore because you can't tie it to anything?

"Well, now I think he was telling me good-bye. That's what that extra weight was, he was saying good-bye."

My own sorrow about Brian is a hard, sharp thing; dislodged from the painful "If only we had known," it quickly settles into "Then what?" Equally uncomfortable. What could we have done? I doubt that we could have helped him; we didn't know then what we know now. Because it is largely a result of Brian's death that Keith and I have learned how to live.

17

Because there had never been a long period in our lives together when there was no excitement or crisis, I had few reference points by which to gauge how Keith and I were doing. Though by the time Keith had been clean for six years, I knew that staying off drugs would never again be a problem for him, though we had deepened our understanding of ourselves and each other, though our relationship had become more placid than it ever had been, it was still more difficult than I wanted it to be.

I knew that Keith had worked terrifically hard in his own therapy; he had put his heart into his AA program, really trying to live the twelve steps as he interpreted them. He had become a sponsor to a man who had just learned he was HIV positive, and Keith was abundantly kind and generous with him. He also tried group therapy and seemed to have new insights about how he functioned in different kinds of relationships. I could see that he was making an effort to change. While he still suffered from migraines, he was treating them with meditation and nonaddictive painkillers. Everything he was doing indicated to me that Keith *wanted* to be happy.

But it seemed an awful struggle. I never knew what kind of mood he would be in the next time I saw him. He might leave the house feeling fine in the morning, and return at night morose, miserable, under the shroud of a black scowl. I got tired of asking him what was wrong. He didn't know. He was exhausted. He was angry. He wished I would leave him alone. He wished everyone would leave him alone.

Though I still might not have been able to articulate what it was I'd been waiting for in our marriage, I knew this wasn't it.

Apart from Keith, I was happy. My friendships were strong. I had taken a full-time editorial job, and I felt appreciated; the staff I supervised was productive and satisfied. Reid, thriving in school, was content, sensitive, happy. But marriage to Keith—it pinched me.

The idea that Keith was depressed again went off like a flashbulb in my head, illuminating all of the dark, random observations I hadn't been able to make sense of. "You know what, I think you're depressed," I told him finally. "Why don't you go back to your psychiatrist?"

"I'm not depressed," Keith said. But living with him was like living with someone who was struggling to keep awake, when what he really wanted was only to sleep, who was irritated by the steady, ordinary throb of every day. Everything seemed too difficult for Keith, any kind of stimulus seemed to hurt him, as if he had a kind of soul-flu. I knew he was sick. I could see it.

It started with my losing Keith's place in a book he was reading. I had picked it up, begun to leaf through it, and been interested enough to flip back to the beginning. I thought I had replaced his bookmark, who knows? I put the book down and forgot about it.

Hours later, I heard Keith grumbling on the other side of the room. That sound was as predictive of a storm as the low, portentous rumble of approaching thunder. "What's up?" I called over to him.

Keith held up the book. The noon sun, blazing in the window behind him, cast a silvery aura that set him in deep shadow. I couldn't make out what book it was.

He punched the air with it. "Were you reading this?"

I shaded my eyes and then took a couple of steps closer to be able to see. Suddenly, the image on the cover swam out of the dark. "Well, yeah," I said, "I looked through it. Why?"

Keith's face tightened in anguish. "You lost my place!" he shouted. "I was reading this book, this was my book, and now you've been reading it and you lost my place!"

I stood very still, trying to figure out if I had missed something, if I had somehow forgotten the disastrous feeling you get when someone has moved your bookmark.

Something began to rise in me. Softly, at first, I felt my heart begin to pound.

"Keith," I said quietly, still not moving.

I wasn't sure what I wanted to say. The thumping in my chest grew harder, louder, distracting me. I began to feel it in my ears, great pounding waves that washed away everything else in my head. All I could hear was the inexorable roar of it. Then one white wave of fury rose in front of my eyes, blinding me to everything but what was written on it in large, capital letters. "KEITH!" I said. "ARE YOU OUT OF YOUR FRIGGING MIND?"

He slammed the book down on a table and stomped angrily toward me. "It's ridiculous!" he shouted. "It's hopeless!"

Then, stopping abruptly, his voice saturated with despair, *"Why can't you understand?"*

The question, ripe with failure, hung in the air. I could feel its mighty tug on my patience, which had been slowly withering for years, and now felt ossified and brittle as a dead twig.

"Why can't I understand?" I repeated, and it was as if my

asking, too, added weight to the question. It was too much. My patience began to splinter; sharp little shards splitting out at first, and then a great, huge, satisfying snap.

I stared at Keith before I knew what had happened. Then it hit me.

"That's it!" I screamed. "That's it! I won't do this anymore! It's over, goddam-fuck-it-all, I'm getting out!" Crying, I ran from the room.

Keith followed me. His eyes were wild. He grabbed me by the shoulders and roughly turned me around to face him. "You have no idea what I'm going through!" he cried. He dropped into a crouch on the floor. He held his head in his hands and tugged on his hair. I stood stiffly in front of him. "But how can I know if you won't tell me?" I said, crying. "I *want* to know, but you won't tell me. And then you're angry at me for not supporting you!

"I'm sick of it!" I shouted. "I'm sick of you! You're sick! This whole fucking thing is sick! I don't even want to look at you anymore!" I restrained myself from kicking him before I ran into our bedroom and slammed the door.

"Oh my God, oh my God, Val, talk to me," Keith cried on the other side of the bedroom door. "Let me in!"

"Go away!"

"Please, please, we need to talk. I need to talk to you. I have to talk to you!"

"Go away!"

"No, I won't go away!" And more urgently, *"I'm not going away!"*

Keith began to talk to me, then; through my sobbing and through the bedroom door I could hear the smooth, deep, continuous chord of his voice, steady and passionate. It was not what he was saying, but finally, the sound of his feelings, that moved me off the bed to open the door and let him in.

The following night, as we sat at the kitchen table after supper, I said to Keith, "We have to talk." I had both my hands flat on the black place mat before me, as if it were a tablet I was going to read from. Keith sat back a bit from the table, hands in his lap.

"Look, I'm very unhappy here," I began. "There's just not enough in this for me to keep trying. I don't know what's happening with you; it doesn't even matter to me anymore whether you're depressed or not. The point is that I don't choose to live with the distance and the anger and the . . . difficulty that I seem to have to live with in order to live with you."

Keith was pale, and he slumped a little in his chair.

Looking at him, I felt sad for both of us. The vinyl place mat glistened as my tears slid onto it off my chin.

"I'm leaving, Keith," I said. "I've been looking at apartments. I'm going to try to be out of here by the end of this month."

"Oh, no," Keith said. "Don't do this. Let's try to work it out, please. What can I do?"

"You can make it easier by cooperating and not fighting it. You can help me financially. You can help me figure out how we should talk to Reid about it.

"And you can see a therapist to help you get a handle on what's troubling you."

Keith got up and came over to where I was sitting. He pulled me up out of my chair and squeezed me. "I love you so much," he said, crying. "I don't want to make you unhappy. And I don't want us to separate. I'll go to see a doctor. Give me a couple of months. If you still want to separate, then I'll move out. It'll be easier on you and Reid.

"Just give me a couple of months," Keith said.

I continued to look at apartments during the weeks that Keith again began seeing the therapist he had worked with during the first three years of his recovery. Once I had made up my mind that I would be happier living on my own, I didn't want to lose my momentum. The more I thought about it, the more appealing the idea became. I imagined each place I saw with my things in it: the piano there, against that wall with the window, my bureau here, a side chair there, by the bed. I looked at a tiny one-bedroom, light sparkling over the white walls, high over the East River; a long, narrow loft with shiny, hardwood floors, begging for a basketball net at each end. And I thought: how luxurious to have my own place, where I set the mood, where I don't walk in wondering whether I'm going to be facing Heathcliff with a headache.

But concurrently, the idea of continuing to live with Keith was becoming more appealing. He was different in a way he had never been before; not exactly happy-go-lucky—he would never be that. But he was lighter, more present, attentive, accessible, more patient. He was wonderful. More wonderful than the Keith I had fallen in love with.

On a sultry evening as we were walking home from the movies, he asked, "Do you notice anything different about me?"

His question took me by surprise; I still must have been thinking about the movie we'd just seen, or what we were going to do for dinner, but I was stuck in the immediacy of the moment, and I thought he meant, did I notice he was wearing new shoes, or he'd got a haircut or something. I studied him for a couple of seconds. "I don't see anything, no," I said. "Why? What do you mean?"

"Well." Keith cleared his throat. We stopped walking. "Well, I've been taking an antidepressant."

℘

Sitting with a work colleague in a sunny plaza one afternoon as we ate our lunch, I tried to describe the way Keith had changed. "It's as if all of his good qualities have come into focus," I said. "And the things that were difficult about him—his moodiness, his temper, the way he focused on his pain—all that has gone into relief.

"It's not as if he's a different person," I said. "Only that I feel as if I'm getting to see the person who has been there all along, who's been obscured by Keith's unhappiness, the person I always knew I loved."

Had I changed my mind, then? my friend asked. Was I still determined to separate?

I don't know, I said, turning my face to the sun and drawing a deep breath. It feels so good right now, as if we're starting something new and fresh.

I closed my eyes. "We'll have to see how it goes," I said.

After a couple of months, Keith stopped taking Zoloft; he said he felt as if it obscured the core of him. But he remained the accessible, considerate person he had become.

Because I was uncomfortable with it, all through the years of Keith's recovery I kept the bulk of my anger at him hidden. I would bring a little of it out at a time, and feel reassured; yep, it was still there, and I could count on it. Then I noticed that whenever I felt that Keith and I were getting close, I found something to get angry at. I said I wanted to be close to him, but now that the opportunity lay before me, I was scared.

There was a problem with my strategy, though. Keith was making an effort to make our marriage work and he was so much more the person I wanted him to be that there was nothing much anymore to hang my anger on. He came home at night, he was clean and was clearly going to stay that way, he was present when he was at home, he was agreeable to most of my demands. Yet many nights, after we had spent what had seemed like a companionable evening reading or talking or watching TV, as I was getting ready for bed I would feel irritation pricking me like an itch. I would look at Keith before I went into the bedroom and make a conscious decision not to say good-night to him. I would leave him reading on the couch, thinking I was washing my face, or getting undressed, and then he'd look up, expecting to see me back in the room with him and I'd be gone, in bed, lights out, the bedroom door shut.

"Why do you do that, hon?" he asked one morning. "Why do you go to bed without saying good-night to me?"

I didn't know. "It doesn't seem important," I'd say. But secretly I was glad I'd hurt him.

I found other ways to exclude him. I lived with him as if I were living alone. If I fixed myself a snack, I would never ask, as he would, "Want some, too?" If I ran to the corner store, I would never ask as he would, "Need anything?"

"Your anger is a land mine," my shrink said to me. "If you don't deal with it, then tomorrow, or next week, or five years down the road, you're going to step on it, it's going to blow up, and it's going to hurt."

It was easy to imagine the injuries. I wanted to be angry; I mean, I wanted to be able to make the choice to be angry, rather than have my anger ambush me, or run me in the sneaky, secretive way that it had. But though I could imagine the anger I had felt when Keith was taking drugs, could remember the hurt his behavior had caused me, I couldn't now summon up any feeling about it. I would say to myself, be angry! And my body would turn to wood.

Through work in therapy, I discovered that if I allowed myself to experience my anger, to acknowledge it, to let it express itself, then I knew on some level that I would eventually want to let go of it, that I wouldn't need it anymore. That was terrifying. Because for a long time my anger had comforted me; it was steady, predictable. I thought I controlled it. I knew what it yielded and its limitations. I used it as a substitute for what I really wanted from Keith. It was always accessible to me; it filled me up. What would happen if I shared it?

My anger needed a dark place to grow; if I shined a light on it, exposed it to the air, it would cower, shrink, lose its power. But I had coddled it, and it grew, took on increasing strength till I wasn't sure anymore what it looked like, how big and hefty it was, what effect it would have if I acknowledged it. Would it take me over?

And there was Keith: he had been through a kind of pain I still couldn't completely imagine. He was pulling through. If I showed him my anger, would he be able to withstand it?

Starting in the therapist's office, but then whenever I chose to call them up, terrible scenes played on the screen in my head. Keith, like Brian, was hit and killed by a truck. Keith was robbed and shot on the street coming home late one night from the studio. I began to insert myself into the drama. I pushed Keith into the path of the truck! I was holding the gun! I no longer was peeking through my fingers to look at the carnage. I was ripping him apart with my bare hands. Standing over him with my foot on his face, pulling his arm out of his socket. I was the Terminator, finally giving my anger some muscle. And when I was through with him, Keith was pulp. It felt great.

Gradually I began to feel a shift; the anger I had used up left room for something else. I wanted to hold (what was left of) Keith in my arms. I needed to tell him that I was angry, and that

I was sorry, too. I needed to tell him that I didn't want to cause him any more pain. That I loved him.

"It's okay," I imagined him saying to me. "I was sick. I'm going to be well. I love you."

A couple of days or a week later, the drama might begin again. The violence. The anger spent. The rapprochement. A little more room for something else. I played it out over and over till I wasn't afraid of it anymore.

I began to feel more generous toward Keith. And I had an easier time telling him how angry he had made me. Since I was no longer keeping my anger secret, feeding it clandestinely, it never had a chance to grow. Each time I let it have a voice, it expired into the air.

With my anger no longer blocking the way, I was able to enjoy a more objective view of Keith. I began to appreciate him in a way I never had. Though those qualities that had originally attracted me to him were the same ones, they were now more apparent than they had ever been. His serious intelligence, his commitment, his perfectionism, his sincerity, and gentleness—all of these things I saw as a kind of nobility in my husband. It seems to me now that as I admired those qualities, Keith grew into them, that the more I appreciated them, the more they appreciated, the more pronounced they became.

Over the next few months I began to feel, unequivocally, that I wanted to be his partner. When I thought about the work he'd done to overcome his depression and his grief, I felt honored to be his friend, honored to be his wife. One day, as we sat at the kitchen table after lunch, I told him so.

As he listened to me, he folded his hands on the table in front of him. He put his head down for a moment, touching his forehead to his thumbs. Then he lifted his head and turned to me. "I am a lucky man," he said.

"Val, I saw a place downtown," Keith said casually one morning as we were dressing for work. "It's a sublet. It's got two bedrooms, so, you know, if we separated, Reid could spend several nights a week with me."

I slipped on my sandals.

"Do you still want me to move out?" he asked. "Should I take it?"

Here is another chance, I thought to myself, here is where you can make the choice again, freely this time, from a position of strength, rather than need, either to be with Keith, or to move on without him. A life apart. Should I take it?

"No," I said. We just stood still for a second, at the foot of the bed, facing each other.

"Can you see the difference in yourself?" I asked. "Do *you* feel different to you?"

"Everything is so much easier," Keith said. "Clearer and easier."

"It's so much easier to love you now," I said. We embraced and kissed.

"I really want us to be together," Keith said. "Do you?"

"Yes," I said. "I do."

I felt as if I were often testing Keith after we had both committed to our marriage. He had been largely absent for the first three years of Reid's life. Now I needed to know: what kind of father was he? I felt that maybe more than anything, his interactions with his son would reveal the person he had become—because for me, responding to our young child evinced both raw reaction as well as my noblest desires to be honest and fair and constant.

I was still reluctant to leave Reid alone with Keith, though I forced myself to, in spite of the fact that they had spent a weekend together in South Carolina, and now often went out together on weekends for errands and such. Of all the things I needed to learn to trust Keith with, including my own vulnerability, learning to trust him with Reid was hardest. I was afraid he would lose him, or neglect him, or forget what he was doing and leave the pilot light burning on the stove. But Keith began to show himself with Reid, to show his understanding, his ability to share what he'd learned.

I was working out on my NordicTrack one weekend morning as Reid, then six, watched cartoons. He became bored and began to whine. Wanting attention, he sauntered over to my machine and began poking at it as I slogged away. I hated that machine. I had just bought it (and would soon sell it) and I was doggedly trying to imagine a virgin Alpine slope. But whenever I opened my eyes, I saw a thick curtain of dust motes floating in the sunshine that beat down into the room. I was hot. It was hopeless.

"Don't do that, Reid," I said, ominously and out of breath. "It's annoying." Van Morrison wailed from the bedroom. Under the hiss of the shower spray, Keith reached for the high notes.

"Why don't you turn off the television and build with your Legos?"

"No thanks," said Reid.

"How about doing a little reading?"

"Dumb idea," Reid said, taking a step closer.

"Well, find something to do, and please do it away from this machine," I said. "Somebody's going to get hurt."

As if he were going to dance, Reid threw up his arms and took a step sideways. But instead of moving away, he lunged toward the machine and hit the mechanism that controlled the skis. It slipped, the skis slid quickly toward the back of the base, and I grabbed onto the main support to keep from falling. "God-damit!" I yelled, and before I knew it, with the flat of my hand I hit Reid on the head.

He was stunned. In his whole life, I had only hit him once before, a halfhearted swat on his diapered behind. For six years I had been repeating to him the mantra of all modern parents, "Use words. Don't hit. Hitting only hurts."

Now I shouted at him. "I am so angry at you! I could have hurt myself! I'm sorry I hit you. Now go to your room!"

He was crying as he slipped behind his bedroom door. "It was an accident," I heard him say quietly, just before the door clicked shut.

After Keith dressed we all sat on the floor in Reid's room. "So what happened?" Keith said.

I was still angry. "Go ahead and tell Daddy," I said to Reid.

"I started to dance, and then by mistake I touched the pole and the rope slipped and then Mom lost control and almost fell," Reid said. "I didn't mean to do it. It was an accident." He wrung his hands and struggled not to cry. "And then Mom hit me."

I looked at Keith and then at Reid. "I believe you," I said. "I'm sorry that I hit you; I felt very angry and I lost control."

We all sat for a few moments. Reid cried softly into a tissue. I felt like crying myself. I felt as if something else needed to be resolved, but I didn't know what it was.

Finally Keith said, "Honey, were you scared?" Reid, crying harder, looked up at Keith.

"Yes," he said.

"I know how you feel," Keith said. "I remember how that feels."

I thought of my father's explosive anger and the fear it engendered in me. "It's lousy," I said.

Keith moved across the floor. He put his arms around Reid. "I love you," he said. Then he stood up and reached for my hand. "Come on, let's get some breakfast," he said, pulling me up. I took Reid's hand and pulled him up, too.

"What'll it be," I said as we walked out of the room, "cereal or pancakes?"

"Pancakes for me!" Keith said dramatically.

"Me, too!" echoed Reid.

"I was talking with a client today," Keith was saying, "and she was complaining about something and all of a sudden I actually heard her. I mean I heard her without my own responses to what she was telling me.

"It was incredible. She was disappointed, she was angry, and when she was through, I said, 'I'm sorry, Barbara.' And I meant it.

"And she just kind of stopped short. 'Thank you for listening to me,' she said. And I said, 'I'm glad I could.'" Keith was shaking his head in disbelief.

"Everything's different now that I'm not responding to people from places I've been hurt before."

"Yeah," I said. "It's a different world, isn't it?"

18

During the years following Brian's death and Keith's illness and recovery, the hardest thing for me was living with the indecision I regularly felt about whether or not I was making a mistake in continuing to work on our marriage. Even once I had decided that I was committed to it, I was haunted by the idea that I might put in years of effort and then realize that I had done the wrong thing. If the marriage was right, wouldn't I know it, wouldn't I feel sure in some deep, incontrovertible way that Keith and I were supposed to be together? During the toughest times, when Keith was getting high, and then afterward when we were distant but were beginning to discover our reasons for having chosen one another, I knew that we had work to do together. I never seriously thought about leaving the relationship then. It was afterward, when we were solidly past the crises, when we had reached a point in the marriage where our course had stabilized and it seemed as if we had shifted into a cruise, when I began thinking, now what? Now that he's not trying to kill himself, and I don't need to have to hold everything together, what exactly do I want? I needed to figure that out, and once I figured it out, I needed to have the guts to tell him. It might have been more appropriate to do this before you were married, I told myself. That's probably what most people do.

Then I had this delightful thought: fuck what most people do.

I wish Keith and I had more fun together with other people. I wish when we went to a party I could admire the way he chatted easily with my friends. I wish he could tell a story; I wish he could tell a joke. I wish he could make the kind of small talk that relaxes people enough to be comfortable talking about bigger things. I wish that he weren't so purposeful about everything.

"I feel different from other people," Keith said over dinner not long ago.

"How so?"

"I don't know," Keith said. "I feel as if I move at a different pace.

"Val, do your friends think I'm odd?"

"You are odd." I saw a faint flicker of hurt in his eyes. "I'm sorry, hon. I mean, you know," I said, "just compared to ordinary people." Keith glanced at me sideways. "You don't put much stock in social convention. So you give off a sense that there are different rules around you. You're quiet when you're with people, and you don't often volunteer what you're thinking.

"You're not exactly an open book," I said. "It's hard to get to know you."

Keith got up from the table to clear the dishes.

"But I love knowing you," I said. He turned and gave me a look.

"Oh, well." He sighed.

"No, really," I said. "You know why you're special? There's not one iota of bullshit in you. You're the truest, cleanest person I've ever met."

On a winter evening when Reid was about seven, the three of us sprawled comfortably on the living room couch. We had gotten into a discussion about *things,* about how people surround themselves with material things and why they like to do that. I think it came up because Reid was in a particularly acute "buy me" stage, and we were trying to give him—and ourselves—some perspective on it. It was a cool discussion, as those discussions went, not fired at the moment by Reid's desire for any specific thing, and we breezed along with it until Keith said abruptly, "I was just thinking of when I sat alone with Brian for the last time at his wake."

I leaned toward his end of the couch. "Brian's wake?" I said.

Keith continued so softly that I had to stay in that position to be able to hear him. "I remember thinking of what Brian was leaving behind," Keith said. "He didn't really own anything. But the kids who came to say good-bye to him seemed to love him so much, and I remember hearing them talking about the good ways that Brian had influenced them and I thought, nothing else is important. In the end we only leave what we've given away."

Reid, leaning against his father, wiped his eyes. I was crying, too.

"Keith, I love you," I said. Feeling afraid that the conversation was too heavy for a seven-year-old, I asked Reid, "Are you okay?"

"Yeah," he said quietly, "just happy-sad." So happy that it's sad, Reid had said once, trying to describe his feeling about God. "Oh, honey," we had told him then, "we know that feeling inside out."

For a long time when I thought about what I wanted from our marriage, I looked to the couples around me, as if I could get a sense of what the possibilities for Keith and me were from what other people seemed to have. The more I looked, the worse I felt.

I learned that it is deadly to compare.

"Jack hasn't had a drink in four years," a friend told me of her husband, whose alcoholism had disrupted their life and who quit one day cold turkey. No regular AA meetings. No depression. No major behavioral changes. "It's wonderful between us," she said of their relationship. They both have demanding jobs; a nanny cares for their four young children. "Drinking just isn't a problem for him anymore.

"It was good before," she told me, "but I never thought it could be this good."

"She's lying," said another friend when I described to her how easy it sounded.

"No, I don't think so," I said.

"Who has a life like that, after fifteen years of marriage they didn't know it could be so wonderful?"

"Some people must," I said doubtfully. "Isn't that what we want when we decide to get married? Isn't that what we all hope for?"

"Yes," said my friend, "it is what we hope for. What we get, on the other hand, is real life. Is your marriage satisfying?"

"It's satisfying, but it's hard work."

"But is it good enough?"

Was it good enough? It didn't meet my expectations about what a marriage should be. I tried to think of couples I knew who had had a marriage that met those expectations. Except for my friend and her husband, I couldn't come up with any. I thought about what it meant to me to have a good enough marriage. Yes, I felt sure that my marriage *was* good enough.

But was good enough good enough for me?

Reid was performing at a gymnastics meet in Massachusetts, and had been driven up there by the family of one of his fellow gymnasts. Keith and I were to follow that evening so that we would be there for the start of the meet the next morning. It would be a long drive; we were to meet at home at six, and leave right away. Almost as soon as I got home, I got sick to my stomach. A few minutes later, Keith walked in with his face screwed up like he'd been staring into an A-bomb. "What happened to you?" I asked, and then answered before he could. "Migraine?"

"The worst," Keith said.

"That's swell," I said. "I feel like I'm going to puke. How're we going to make this drive?" The idea of neither of us being there for Reid's meet—his first—made me feel terrible.

"Let's lie down for an hour," Keith said. "Maybe you'll feel better then, too." We waited one hour, then two, then three.

"It's now or never," I said, at ten o'clock.

"Let's go," said Keith.

Partly to keep each other awake, and partly because we so rarely had three hours to ourselves uninterrupted by work or child or other commitments, we talked the whole way. In the hotel room, I hung up our jackets and unpacked my stuff while Keith poked around. "Say, classy. Coffee machine in there," he said, pointing back with his thumb as he emerged from the bathroom. I turned down the bed and looked at him. It was the middle of the night and we were in a strange town, in a cruddy hotel room paved in beige, punctuated by the kinds of paintings bad dreams are made of—the kind of place that makes me feel lonely and uprooted, but still, I felt comfortable. Keith was there. It was us against the decor.

"Which side, hon?" he asked.

It was cool in the room and we undressed quickly, slipped into bed, and turned out the light. Keith felt for my head and kissed me good-night. Then he turned away from me and I scooted up against his back. I put my arm around him and pulled myself to him. He covered my hand with his. He was warm and solid, familiar, an anchor in a strange bed. As I floated off to sleep, I thought: yes, this is good enough for me.

Three years ago, for his birthday, I decided to buy Keith a ring. He didn't like to wear jewelry, so I found a ring as delicate as the white-gold sliver of a new moon. Would he wear it? I didn't care. I bought it because I wanted him to know that I loved him; I wanted him to see the ring as a symbol of our commitment. I had begun wearing my wedding ring on my ring finger, and liked it there. Let him wear his on a keychain, I thought, if that's what he wants; it's a token of my love for him.

On the day I bought it we were visiting San Francisco, and I had the ring delivered to the hotel. It was at the desk when we returned from an evening out. "What's this?" Keith asked, feeling the package on our way up to our room. "Oh, I know what this is," he said, eyes sliding suspiciously over to me.

Inside the room, I sat on the bed while Keith opened the package, looking grimmer and grimmer with each tear of the wrapping. He popped open the small black box silently. Then he looked up at me and said, "Why did you do this?"

I had a couple of questions of my own. Why couldn't you just say thank-you? Or how about, I don't know what to make of this?

"I bought the ring because I love you, and I wanted to show you that I do," I told him. Then I went into the bathroom, shut the door, and stood in front of the marble sink. I dimmed the lights till there was only a pretty pink glow. I stared into the mirror. I thought I looked like a child who'd been bitten by a familiar dog. "Oh, fuck," I said. "What an idiot." Meaning him.

Three years ago I might have stormed out of that bathroom, grabbed the ring, and told Keith to screw himself. That night I took a deep breath. I am going to stay open through this, I told myself; I'm going to stay with my original feeling for Keith. His response hurt me, but it doesn't change my intention. If he doesn't want to keep the ring, I will keep it, because I want to remember what I felt when I bought it . . . and, yes, what I felt when he received it.

In spite of feeling hurt, I actually felt happy, too.

After a few minutes I turned off the light and went back into the room, which was quiet and dark. As soon as I climbed into bed, Keith reached for me. I slid down next to him. As he caressed my face, I felt the cool sliver of gold against my cheek. "I'm sorry, honey," Keith said. "I'll get used to it. I love you."

19

Sometimes, when I'm looking at Keith, I see Brian. He emerges from Keith's features, the way the profiles emerge from the black and white optical trick that looks at first like two Grecian columns. And in the same way that you can't make the trick happen—that it only works when you relax your eyes and stop searching for a different image—that's the way I see Brian in Keith's face. It takes me by surprise. In the instant it takes for Keith's expression to change, it's gone.

I always mention it to Keith. "You looked exactly like Brian just then," I'll say, or "I just saw Brian in your face."

Keith'll go "hunh," and then we'll both be silent for a moment as we remember. I think I romanticize what our relationship with Brian might have been. I forget how difficult it was to talk to him most of the time, how I often felt irritated by the superficiality of our conversations. In my fantasy of how things would be now if he were alive, he has grown along with Keith, shed the constricting skin of his limitations, and triumphed over his addiction. He and Keith would talk often, he would come for dinner, be one of our family, play ball with Reid.

But always I come back to this pivotal question: how would Keith and I have changed if Brian were still with us?

And then I feel grateful to Brian, and sorry, and wish he could know what a gift for his brother, and for me, came to us in part because he died.

Though Keith's family all told me that they were afraid after Brian died that Keith would also kill himself, I don't remember any of them expressing that fear to me at the time. I think I would have dismissed it. What his family saw was that Keith was addicted to cocaine, just as Brian had been. Why would his outcome be any different?

"What saved me was that I had hope," Keith says. "Even when I was in the most pain."

He grew up without religion. On a ski club trip in the Canadian Rockies when he was about twelve, he remembers riding between train cars and seeing towering, white-capped mountain peaks jutting majestically into the cerulean sky. "God!" he said, not as an exclamation, but because something had run through him. He knew then, he says, that he harbored a connection to something larger than himself. Brian was searching, Keith believes, for that feeling. He believes that the need to connect with a larger self was what both he and Brian—and maybe all addicts—were seeking through drugs.

"You know, I've changed my mind," Keith said, casually, a couple of years ago. "I'm not sure at all that Brian killed himself." On a weekend evening, we were getting dressed to go out.

I was pulling on a turtleneck and stopped, surprised, with my head popped out of the knit collar and the arms flung over my shoulders. "What do you mean?"

"I mean I don't believe he jumped in front of a truck," Keith said as he moved about the room, collecting the change from the dresser, a few business cards, a pen, and dropping them into his pockets. "I think he was confused; I think he was trying to run across the road; I think the truck took him by surprise."

Keith had said once or twice before that he wasn't sure that

Brian had committed suicide, that he thought maybe he had shot up, was very high, and miscalculated the speed of the truck, that he had wanted only to sprint across the road. But why?

"People do irrational things when they're high," Keith said.

Brian shoots up a gram of coke. He has tried to quit and can't, and now, even when he boots, all he can feel is the unrelenting pain of self-betrayal. He kicks off his sneakers and pulls off his socks, sopping with perspiration, and drops them heavily into a wet pile on the floor. His shirt, too, is soaked; he yanks it over his head. Sweat flies off it like sparks. His body is bleeding water. Now he is starting to crash.

He has gotten into his car because he is going to kill himself. He is going to drive his car into a wall and end this hell.

He takes the small dark streets at a reckless sixty, slowing down only for turns. He hits the open highway, pushing the accelerator to the floor. There's a concrete abutment coming up fast, sooner than he remembered. He flicks on the high beams so that he can see the wall. It expands so quickly, it seems to shake in front of him.

Seconds before he is about to hit, there is a reflex, or loss of courage, or change of heart, and he jerks the wheel so that the car swerves slightly, slamming into the wall, but not head-on.

Brian has hit his head. He's dazed and sick. He kicks the door open with his bare foot, pulls himself out of the car.

Leaving the door open, he moves away, lurching a little, down a shallow gully and up an embankment. His feet sink into the soft grass, slowing him down. When he reaches the highway, the hard slap of pavement causes a quickening; his leg is hurting, but he speeds up his pace, breaks into a limping jog. He crosses lanes, head down, his eyes closed.

Slowly he becomes aware of a distant rumbling from behind. The rumbling rolls nearer, Brian runs faster, but it's overtaking him, he can feel the shaking thunder in the road and the cool breath of an eighteen-wheeler tickling his back. There is still time to get out of the way.

Suddenly, the truck sounds its horn, startling him, three violent blasts, each one louder, longer, more urgent. Which way? Which way? *Which way?*

In an instant, a shadow freezes in the bright white of the headlights' glare. A second later, the impact sends it flying, like a ghost-figure, over the shiny snout of the grille. Quickly, airily, it disappears, sucked into the receding black of the road.

"Keith," I asked one night recently, "do you miss your brother?"

"No," Keith said. "I don't really miss him. I knew a long time ago that I would be able to live with Brian's death. I knew I would be all right when I began to allow myself to feel the grief.

"Because when I was able to grieve, I was also able to feel how much I loved Brian. And then I knew that my love for him would always be there, even if he wasn't."

Keith said then that Brian's girlfriend had told him after he died that one night Brian had ridden into the city on his motorcycle, desperate for help, for a way out of his addiction. Keith imagined him as he sat on his bike outside our building, looking up, struggling with the idea of confessing everything to Keith and surrendering his isolation. But his disease, his addiction, was telling him Keith wouldn't understand, that he would condemn his weakness, telling him that sharing his secret desperation would somehow make his disgrace real and seal his fate to it. If he were ever going to be a man, he would have to rely only on himself, as their father had taught them.

"That vision of him, sitting on his bike, alone in the dark, knowing he was approaching his own destruction and unable to ask for help . . ." Keith paused. "It's a sad metaphor for everything that kept us both fixed in our unhappiness." He closed his eyes.

"What a terrible thing for Brian," said Keith, "that the simple act of sharing his weakness carried such huge, insurmountable shame."

"Oh, love," I said.

"I wish I could share with him who I am now," Keith said.

On the wing of that wish, Keith sailed back into the rehab community.

"I need to be able to give some of this back," he said one evening not long ago as we lay in bed reading. "I've gotten so much help over the last seven years. I want to give some help now."

"What do you want to do?" I asked. "I mean, how?"

Keith laid his book facedown on the quilt. "I'm not sure," he said thoughtfully. "I think I want to train to be a drug counselor or get into social work, or something. I think I might have the capacity to help people who are going through what I've been through. Anyway, I want to try."

In the following weeks, Keith made some calls. He talked with the counselors at the rehab he'd been in. He entered a training program connected with the hospital and spent a series of weekends learning how to be a group facilitator. After his training, he would be qualified to lead a group of "graduates" of the rehab and their partners.

"I feel as if I know how to do this," he said after the first meeting of his group. "It's hard, but I'm learning from it, too."

Every Tuesday night he meets with his group. Their stories, their experiences are both familiar and hard to believe.

"Some of these addicts seem so manipulative," Keith said one night after his meeting. I had been reading the paper at the kitchen table; Keith was lying on the couch, and I couldn't see him. "Was I manipulative when I was taking drugs?"

"No," I said, putting down the paper and remembering. I felt a twinge of anger. "You were mean and irresponsible. And scared." It still felt good to tell him directly.

I stood up so that I could see him. He lay with his arms behind his head, gazing up at the ceiling. Looking at him, it felt as if the person I was remembering was not the same person I was talking to now, but instead someone we had both known well. I knew that that was because Keith had changed. But it wasn't only because he had changed. I had, too. I had learned to become forgiving, and it was the light of that forgiveness that illuminated Keith, that allowed him to show me the parts of himself that I had grown to love. So it was partly because I perceived him differently that he had become a different person.

I looked over at him and felt proud. We had worked hard to stay together. I thought how sad it might have been if I had left him.

"I wonder what would have happened," I said.

"If what?"

"I wonder what would have happened if we had split up then," I said.

"I would have died," Keith said.

Keith continued to maintain his interest in Meher Baba, and became active in the small community of Baba followers in New York City.

So when Bhau, one of Meher Baba's mandali—the inner circle of disciples—came from India to the States to visit and to see followers here, Keith made an appointment to see him. I had never met him, but Keith had, and wanted to see him again; on a bright August afternoon he went uptown to meet with him. Keith spoke with Bhau, talked with him about a few things, when suddenly Bhau asked, "Where is your wife? Is your wife not coming up to see me?"

"My wife?" Keith said, confused. He had only mentioned to me in passing that he had arranged to see Bhau, assuming correctly that I wasn't interested. He couldn't imagine why Bhau would ask for me. "Well, she's home, and she, she didn't say anything about coming up."

"But I must see her!" the disciple cried. "Tell her to call to make an appointment! Call her now!"

Keith, mystified, called me. I was writing a magazine story.

"Val, Bhau wants to see you," Keith said.

"He wants to see me? What for?"

"I don't know. He just said he wants you to come up whenever you can."

This is insane, I thought. The guy is trying to play a trick on Keith at my expense. "Tell him I'm sorry but I can't come," I said. "Tell him I'm on a deadline."

Keith was silent a moment. "Are you sure?" he said.

"Yes."

A few minutes later, the phone rang again. Keith was laughing nervously. "He wants to come down to see you," he told me. "Whenever you can spare a little time."

"What the heck for?" I said. "Does he know something I don't know? What, am I going to be hit by a bus or something? Does he know I'm not a follower?"

"I already told him," Keith said. "It's not important to him."

The next day, late morning, our elevator discharged a motley group: about five or six Westerners and a small, sixtyish, balding, round-bellied Indian man in a short-sleeved shirt, polyester pants, and suspenders. As he stepped out of the elevator, he opened his arms wide to me. "There you are, my sister," he said, smiling broadly. He embraced me. I was more than a head taller than he and felt awkward as I leaned into him. "Oh, yes, yes, yes!" he said after he pulled away and stood, still smiling, looking at me. He bobbed his head a little with each "yes!" from side to side. He reached up and held my chin and looked happily into my eyes. "Oh, yes," he said again. "Let's have a talk."

We left the group, Keith among them—he had come home from the studio thinking he might help the meeting go smoothly—in the front of the house and I led Bhau down the hallway to our living room. He walked over to the sofa, put his hands on his knees as he sat down, rolling back a little into the cushions, and patted the seat next to him. I sat. He stared at me and smiled. I smiled back. He stared some more and smiled some more, shaking his head the way you might when you see something you can't quite believe is really there.

It was warm in the living room and I began to sweat. "So," I said, finally. He continued to look at me. "So, what's new?"

"Ah, yes, very good, very good. What's new." Bhau looked around the room and out the windows. "Everything is new, isn't that so? Everything!"

I thought he expected an answer, so I said, "Well, I guess so." Then, not wanting to be dishonest, because though I thought I knew what he meant, I wasn't completely sure, I said,

"Well, in a way, it is. Well, that's certainly one way of looking at it." I didn't want to hurt his feelings.

I think I asked him then why he wanted to see me.

"You are my sister," he said. "When I am traveling to different cities around the world there are several people I am always sure that I am seeing."

"Huh," I said. "But what draws you to them?"

Bhau shrugged, as if the question had no relevance. Then he touched my cheek. "Love God wholeheartedly," he said.

"Yeah, okay," I said, "sure."

But something was creeping up on me as Bhau talked, as if his voice were a background sonata, a musical cue, dipping and swelling, that was leading me into . . . what? As I sat there listening to him, suddenly I realized: it was relief. Huge, monstrously beautiful, safe, and complete. There was only one thing in the world that I would ever need to know, and I had already discovered it. The real, shimmering, incontrovertible truth, the constant compassionate presence—the love—I yearned for was in me, and all around me, and would always be. I wept.

Bhau took both of my hands in his. He said some things I couldn't understand because of his Hindi accent, so I had to keep asking him to repeat himself: "What? Sorry, what?" But he said everything as if he were saying it for the first time, as if he could never lose patience, as if everything were a small revelation. He exuded beatitude.

After a while Bhau said, "Well!" with a kind of finality I took to mean that our interview was over.

"Ready to go?" I said. I blew my nose and then got up to call the rest of the group to join us. There were a few minutes of uncomfortable conversation before someone reminded Bhau that he had to be back uptown for his next appointment. As Keith ushered him down the hall to the elevator, I heard Bhau say something to him that made Keith laugh and turn back to look at me strangely. "He said I didn't have to worry," Keith told me later. "He said, 'She's one step ahead of you.'"

This, of course, bewildered and annoyed Keith, who took his spiritual commitment very seriously. Wasn't he the one doing the spiritual reading, making the effort to surrender himself to God? He was trying! How could I, who seemed so rooted in the real world, in my fears and needs and desires, be a step ahead of him?

I caught Keith regarding me differently, as if he had taken a new interest in me. "Your wife," Bhau said to Keith. "Look!"

Over the course of the next few months I asked myself, what was that all about? My practical instincts were to try to find a reason for Bhau's visit, but I just couldn't come up with a motivation. One of my friends suggested that the Baba "group" was trying to co-opt me. But there was no "group," and, though the thought had occurred to me as well that Bhau was, for his own reasons, trying to persuade me to believe that Meher Baba was God, that explanation didn't feel right at all: he didn't really seem to care. Instead, I found myself focusing on how I felt when Bhau was with me, and what I thought about after. Months before I met Bhau, I had become more open to all experience, I realized, than I ever had been since I was a child. Which isn't to say that I had lost my judgment—only that I might choose to suspend it. The connections I made with my friends felt deep and enduring. Even the briefest connections often had a different quality to them; in sharing my authentic, undisguised self, I was making connections real.

And that feeling of relief—it never completely left me. The intensity might increase or decrease, but the constancy and the soundness has never changed.

Keith understands this perfectly.

20

What story do the photographs tell? One of them is twelve years old. Keith sits uncomfortably on the end of a hospital bed. He looks ragged, edgy, fatigued. His dark hair, the dark blue of his sweater, are tinged with a blur, as if he's been moving fast, as if he might rush out of the picture at any instant, leaving only the wavy lines of an image too quick to be caught. But he can't run. In the crook of one arm he cradles a baby, a newborn wrapped in a white hospital blanket, luminescently pale, asleep. The baby's head lolls back slightly against his arm. Its fragility is commanding, weighting him to the spot.

Ten years later, another picture. Keith and Reid, both in dark sweaters, sitting in an instant-photo booth before a light blue pleated curtain. It is a photo they are taking for me, for Mother's Day. They squeeze onto the small metal stool. "Here, Reid," says Keith, "sit on my knee." Keith pulls Reid down gently, tells him to brush his bangs from his eyes. He feeds a bill into the machine. "Ready?" he says. They look into the camera's eye, assuming exactly the same pose.

A bright pop of light, and the machine gurgles, digesting the image. My husband and son wait, trying to blink back their sight.

"I'll take it out, I'll take it out," Reid says excitedly as the photograph slips out of the machine's thin metal lips. He holds it carefully; he and his father gaze at it as the dense grayish-green fog slowly lifts and their faces emerge.

What is it that I love about this picture? That my husband and my son look happy; more than happy. Keith, especially, seems to glow with contentment. Reid's sure, straightforward glance dignifies the childish curve of his cheek; he is not quite smiling. His expression perfectly suits his father's: it's younger, more expectant, budding, as compared to Keith's wide-open gaze. Their faces are bright, and close. Their skin and their hair are just the same color, and though I can see Keith in the shape of Reid's face, I can see myself, too.

I look at them, and I know that they're mine. The alliance between Keith and me feels nearly as physical as the connection I have to my son.

"You didn't have any idea what it was like for me when you were getting high?" I was incredulous. Keith had just finished reading my manuscript and had emerged from the bedroom.

He came over to where I sat, and kissed me. I could see that he'd been crying. He said, "Remember, it's your story." Then he sat down next to me. The one thing that struck him, he said, was that it had been so difficult for me during the months preceeding his recovery, when he was taking drugs.

"I just never understood that it had been so hard for you," he said. The way I had felt at that time—all of that was news to him.

I thought about how what he was telling me now had affected his behavior. He never saw more than what he was going through, never knew how frightened and sad I was. I remembered that Christmas afternoon in the rehab, when he had presented me with the present of antique pins. I wished I had been able to tell him then what I was feeling, tell him that I wanted him to get better, that I wanted us to be a family, that I wanted to learn how to love him. I wondered, if I had been able to take that risk, would he have been able to respond? Would it have made it easier on us if one of us had been able to be open about what we felt?

It makes a difference now. I still will sometimes fall into an old pattern when I'm angry, clamming up rather than saying what I'm feeling, allowing a frost to settle in the air between me and Keith. Used to be, Keith would disappear when he saw that coming on, would retreat into his own defensive anger, ready to strike back as soon as I made the first hit. He doesn't do that anymore.

"It's cool in here," he might say. "What's going on?"

"Nothing. I don't know."

Then he'll look at me. For all I know, he might be thinking about what he wants for lunch, but I read a lot into his look. It says, let's keep this moving along straight and fair; let's be honest; let's not let anger take over; let's look at it, put it out here between us. I remember my sense of responsibility to myself and to Keith. And then, everything changes. There's a silent agreement between us: if one of us can stay open, so will the other. This works because one of us—not necessarily the same one—always is able to stay open. In that way we share our responsibility.

Keith is much more often the one who keeps us on the straightaway.

He was climbing up the subway stairs as I waited on the corner to cross the street. I knew I had seen him somewhere before, but I couldn't place him. Two blocks later we stood at another corner waiting for the light.

"Excuse me, I know you," he said.

I turned to get a better look at him. He was middle-aged, but boyish, in a plaid jacket and chinos. "Yes, I think so."

"You used to go to the Al-Anon meetings at the church up the street."

"Oh, yes, of course!" Suddenly his face took on a different

look: attentive, vulnerable. As if from the other side of the room, I saw him sitting quietly in the metal church chair, thoughtful and unassuming, against the mullioned window.

"Well! How are you?" I asked. He looked good.

"We're doing very well," he said. "We have a daughter; did we have a daughter then? I don't think so. We adopted.

"How's your husband? And your son? You have a son, right?"

I was surprised he remembered. "We're all well, too," I told him. I felt a rush of gratitude. The light changed and we walked.

"That was a difficult time for me," I said. "Al-Anon was really important in helping me get through."

"I feel the same way," he said.

"It gave me a new way of seeing things when I needed it most," I said. "I learned things in those rooms that changed how I relate to the world. It really helped me." I couldn't believe what I was saying to him, but I knew he'd understand.

We had stopped walking.

"Me, too," he said, shaking his head.

"Do you still go?"

"No. Not for years."

"Me neither." We stood facing each other on the sidewalk.

"Well," he said. "I turn off here. It was good seeing you again." He took my hand and grasped it.

"Likewise," I said.

As he walked away, I realized that I didn't know his name. Nor could I remember the names of many of the people whose stories I listened to and who listened to my story during the years I went to Al-Anon meetings. But they weren't strangers. Though I had no desire to continue my conversation with the man I had just encountered, my feeling of connection to him persisted. It was as if I had practiced, with him and with the other people I saw regularly in meetings, how to show my real feelings, my real self, not the one I thought the world expected to see.

No one there ever told me that what I felt was wrong.

Back from a long weekend in Canada with Reid to visit my friend Lou and her two boys, I'm glad that Keith is at home when we get in. It is an early summer afternoon, hot, but not yet the stifling heat of a city July.

"Let's go out to dinner," says Keith, "to that place Reid likes in Little Italy." Reid whoops at the idea.

"Just let me unpack," I say, heading toward the bedroom. I'm hanging up my jacket in our closet. Turning to set something down, I see that there is a string of small presents laid out across my dresser like a loose chain: three cards of beautiful old buttons . . . a perfect little lavender glass with a delicate pattern cut into the sides . . . a filmy black handkerchief embroidered in each corner with a dainty white flower.

"Oh! What's this!" I'm exclaiming, while Keith continues to putter around in the living room. I picture his shy smile when he hears my pleasure and surprise.

"Just some things I found for you," he says, coming into the bedroom. "Some things I thought you'd like."

"I love them. You were thinking of me."

"Of course," Keith says. He kisses me.

"I have something for you, too," I say. Out of my pocket I pull a key ring, KEITH emblazoned in gold on one side, and a colorful, primitive drawing of Niagara Falls on the other.

"Oh my God," Keith says, taking it in his palm and looking it over. "It's awful!" He laughs.

"It had your name on it, honey," I say.

Keith and Reid and I were sitting at the kitchen table, looking over the photographs we had taken during our recent trip to Paris and India. We were laughing at how Reid, at ten, in his Atlanta Braves baseball cap, oversized T-shirt, and shorts seems to have trekked clear across Paris and the subcontinent without ever looking as if he'd left home. Keith sat next to me, his arm around the back of my chair, as we sorted through the photographs of the three of us in India. There was Reid, leaning into the wind on the Deccan Plateau, the flat patchwork of grassy plains in fuzzy muted shades of grays and greens behind him; Keith and me peering out of one of the Ajanta caves, two bright green parrots sailing past us in a psychedelic blur. There was a picture of the pilgrim center where we had stayed, and I remembered kneeling at Meher Baba's tomb and experiencing a wash of compassion and relief, more powerful even than what I'd felt with Bhau, and knowing that it didn't matter what precipitated that feeling, that it was real, that I would simply accept it for the irreplaceable gift that it was.

I leaned over to Keith, to plant a kiss on his cheek, and closed my eyes. As my lips touched his skin, I fell into a swirl of emotion. I wasn't only kissing Keith, the present Keith who was in the room with me, but the little boy Keith, too, who with his brother had stayed in one spot till his aunt told him he could move, and the Keith who had cried in the car that night after he had collected his brother's things, and the Keith who had sat with his brother for the last time at his wake. I was kissing the Keith who told me he loved me when neither of us knew what it meant, as well as the Keith who loved me and who I loved fully now. And I was kissing the brother in Keith, too, as I thought of Brian sitting downstairs alone, on his motorcycle, in the dark.

I willed him to come up, come up! and in his leather jacket and jeans he floated off his bike and slowly rose, like an angel all in black, to our floor. Pulling away from Keith, I looked down at the photograph I was holding. There, standing on a rock at the foot of a verdant hill in India, stood Brian, in a typical Brian pose, leaning forward into the camera, face up, confident and strong. Keith saw him, too.

"What is this?" he asked as he took the picture from my hand. "Wow," he said, staring at the photograph and shaking his head. "It's me."

"Let me see," said Reid, coming around to our side of the table. Then, "It's just Dad," he said.

But as I looked at the photograph, the face continued to change: Brian, Keith, Brian, Keith. I knew that as long as we continued to remember him, Brian would always be with us.

"I was thinking about one of the weekends we spent in the country before we were married," Keith said recently. "Remember the photograph I took of you walking down that path in the woods? What I saw in you then, that's what I was in love with."

A late fall weekend; we had driven up to the Adirondacks to get out of the city. In an old inn, sprawling, stately and anonymous, we rented a room with a fireplace. There was no progress to the days. We walked in the woods, lay on the grass in the warmth of the autumn sun, made love in front of the fire.

"I thought I was in love with you then," I said. "But I didn't even know you. I was just projecting all of the things I wanted a man to be onto you and hoping they'd stick. And all of the things I liked about you, I liked because I wanted those qualities for myself. I thought that by being with you, they'd kind of rub off on me. Or maybe reflect on me, so that I could have them."

Keith nodded. "I thought being with you would make me a better person," he said. "A bigger person, more complete."

I knew what Keith meant. "But that is what happened," I said, "to both of us. We did become more complete."

"Just not in the way we expected."

We were standing in the kitchen; I had returned from dropping Reid off at school. Keith was collecting some papers he needed to take over to the studio. It was the day before our twelfth wedding anniversary. I had put water on for coffee, and leaned against the counter as we spoke.

"What I thought I felt for you then—what was it? It seems so different from what I feel now," I said.

"But there was always something there," Keith said, coming around the counter to stand beside me. "Something I saw in you that was pure, then, untouched by the accumulation of our experiences together. I've been seeing that in you again now, something captured in that picture. . . .

"Don't most people get married because they feel their partner will make them more complete? And then they're disappointed because after a while they don't feel more complete, they begin to feel isolated?"

I thought about that. "Do you?" I asked Keith. "Ever feel isolated anymore?" He looked at me.

"No," he said.

"Me neither." I could think of nothing I couldn't discuss with him and know that eventually, he'd understand.

"So what do you want for us?" I asked.

There was no hesitation in Keith's voice. "I want us to be able to keep growing together, to support each other, to be happy together," he said.

He took my hands in his. "What I saw in you that weekend," he said, "what I see in you still, it's, I don't know . . ." His eyes filled up and he embraced me hard. I cried into the collar of his jacket.

"I love you, Val," Keith said. He continued to hold me tightly.

"It's not at all what I expected," I said, looking up at him and wiping my eyes with the back of my hand.

The real thing, I thought, what a surprise: it doesn't feel evanescent or ephemeral, winding around us like silk, like a breeze, ticklish and exciting; that was what I thought love was. What Keith and I shared—it felt stout, solid, plain, and grand.

I didn't wonder anymore why we were married. We had chosen one another because we had needed one another to understand what we couldn't understand alone. We had effected change in one another, clumsily, without knowing what we were doing. And in spite of that, in spite of not understanding that we had a purpose for each other, we had accomplished it. We had helped each other, and it was painful, but we had learned how it was possible to be happy alone and together.

All of what I had learned from my parents and from our culture about love—it was really about illusion, the illusion of romantic love, it was about falling in love, not about loving. With Keith, I learned what loving is. I had always wanted to be with someone extraordinary, someone who could live up to the mythic proportions of my childlike estimation of my father. And so I courted men who would give me some kind of drama; often the drama generated from the fact that they were still involved with another woman, and so there was conflict built into our relationship from the start. I avoided real love through that drama, because it didn't require feelings, only that my lover and I play the necessary roles. But because of my experience with Keith and with our son, I learned to recognize and to accept the exquisite in the ordinary, to appreciate how awesome and moving and satisfying it could be. It was with Keith and with Reid that I learned how to be in a state of loving, instead of being in love, or demanding to be loved. Between Keith and me, there's little disillusionment, because we see each other, rather than projections of what we wished one another would be.

Keith's dark side still saddens me. And my anger over our past still flares up, surprising me, like the rebel pop and spark that suddenly leaps off the embers of a dying fire. But it's often when we've revealed to one another what is least comfortable that we feel closest.

I think love is an energy all its own that is always there, that moves through us, whenever we are willing to be open to it.

Standing in the kitchen, I took Keith's face in my hands. *I will walk on this feeling all the way to the end of my heart*, I thought, *and still there will be more.*

Valerie Monroe has been an editor at *Ms., Redbook,* and *Self* magazines among others, and has written for many national magazines, including *Parenting, Entertainment Weekly,* and *Mirabella.* She lives in New York City with her husband and son.